Save Casn

The Secrets of Building Wealth

A Guide to Financial Security and Stability

Kevin D. Powell

Atlanta, GA

2012

Library of Congress Cataloging in Publication Data

Save Cash
ISBN-13: 978-0615635422
ISBN-10: 0615635423

To contact the author send an email to 1kevindpowell@gmail.com.

Blog: www.kdpowell.wordpress.com

Twitter: kdpowell

About the author

Kevin loves helping humanity. He is a proud father and devoted husband. He enjoys mentoring young people and giving of his time to help others. He has worked in corporate America for over 13 years and has experience as an entrepreneur. He was born in Norfolk, VA and raised in North Carolina. He attended Northampton County Public Schools System and attended college at North Carolina Central University. He is working towards obtaining a master's degree in Organization Development and Leadership. Kevin volunteers in the community with the United Way, Shoes for Africa and Big Brother & Big Sister Organization. He has volunteered to help the 21st Century Leadership organization and Boys and Girls Club of America.

Dedication

This book is dedicated to my wife Jaime, my four children: Seiana, Eden, Evan, and Brianna, my nephews: Jameel, Taevon, and Alrico, my parents: Joe and Gail, my step-parents: Hernell and Michael, my brothers and sisters: Maurice, Joe, Jr., Lakisha, Shawanda, and Michele, my deceased grandparents: Alice, Harding, Estell, Raymond, and Mattie, my uncles, my aunts, my cousins, my mentees: Corey, Brandy, and Darren and my friends: Sehu, Quray, Walt, Tim, Terry, Eric, Erva, Njathi, Devin M. and Devin B.

Special acknowledgment and honor to:

Jaime Powell, Wife

Quray Bey, Financial Planner

Devin Brown, Credit Counselor

SAVE CASH
The Secrets of Building Wealth
A Guide to Financial Security and Stability

TABLE OF CONTENTS

TABLE OF CONTENTS

"To be satisfied with little is the greatest wisdom, and they that increase their riches increase their cares. But a contented mind is a hidden treasure and trouble finds it not."
Kemetic proverb

"If you wish your conduct to be perfect, to be free from all that is evil, guard against the vice of greed for material things." Sage Ptah Hotep

INTRODUCTION

Data show Americans spending is out of control and it seems to be gaining momentum. In 2012 and beyond, mobile commerce will launch endlessly and target customers strategically through the smart phone revolution. There will be an application for every major retailer and mom and pop shop in the country to get us to spend money.

I am sharing information that came from personal experiences, published articles and books, and testimonies from family members, friends and strangers. It is appalling to hear their struggles with managing money and inability to save because of taking risks on acquiring what they thought would make them happy if they lived through their desires instead of using their better judgment.

A book like this can cover many areas of saving money. I will focus on some key areas that have the potential to set a person on a positive course for the rest of their life. Building wealth will be relative to each individual idea of financial security. The aim would be for the information to perpetually have a positive influence on future generations. Within three generations wealth can be significantly established through consistently saving and investing in an IRA at the maximum allowed amount with an 8 -11% annual return. A more rapid succession to millionaire status is through rising to the rank of senior executive or Chief Executive Officer (CEO), Chief Operations Officer (COO), and or Chief Financial Officer (CFO) of a multi-million or billion dollar company.

For many years I earned over six figures in salary which did not include bonus and a company car. Despite earning a high salary I poorly managed the money I brought home because I had not learned the secret principles of saving money that I am about to share. Many wealthy people will echo that "money makes money." Fortunately, I did place 8-10% of my salary into a 401k plan for a number of years, which it eventually accumulated over six figures. Where I was lacking was saving liquid cash to create wealth. Financial gurus say purchasing land is a good long-term investment, which it is not a liquid investment that can be sold immediately in the case of an emergency or a need for cash; albeit, I would have to agree it is a good long-term investment if cash is not needed right away.

A 401k is good for retirement but not when you need cash immediately; if you take money out of the 401k you have to repay it in the form of a loan to yourself or pay a penalty for early hardship withdrawal. We perish because of lack of knowledge and people are constantly looking for ways to take advantage of our perceived and systematic ignorance about money. It's no fun living paycheck to paycheck; you should not but yourself in that situation. Parents should instill in their children the necessity to save as much money as they can. There's no harm in saving 25-50% of your salary. Where there is a will, there is a way to accomplish it. It may take creativity but anything is possible when you have the mindset and the steadfastness to do it.

When you do not have money saved, it's hard to get a head in life, quit a job you do not like or be able to contribute substantially to a worthy cause. It is easier to quit a job when you have money saved instead of being dependent on a company to provide for you. Many people work for bosses that they do not like or the boss can be unappreciative and horrible to work for. Working and earning a paycheck is something you have to do day in and day out unless you are born into one of the families that believed in passing down generational wealth and sound money principles and disciplines. If not, you should plan to work in a career you enjoy and save money consistently. Eventually, you will have enough money saved to call it quits at work or retire early. When you reach that point in life you will be glad you saved and spent wisely.

People dream of winning the lottery hoping it will help them leave their jobs. Lottery winners and celebrities go broke all the time because of their lack of knowledge about money management and uncontrollable appetite for spending. It is a recurrent cycle of redistribution of wealth back to the wealthy. It is best to have cash and buoyancy, then debt and a heavy burden.

The reality is we live in a new economic era based on global economic uncertainty and face a higher cost of living and inflation. Therefore, it's best to start learning about money as early as possible. Children learn what they are taught and what's reinforced. Many people have accomplished success in life after being educated at a very young age. If they can learn at a young age and go on to do great things in life, so can all young people with guidance. If young people are taught to plan for the future, they will be light years ahead of their counterparts that are not taught that.

When young people start to make a good salary, they should be in a position to save instead of paying the money out to bills. People can easily get stuck in the mud of debt at a young age and then wish they would have saved or been taught about money throughout their childhood and into their early thirties and forties as their income continues to climb to reach a high level.

Young men and women should be careful not to give birth to children at a young age and then be subject to poverty and/or paying child support. Statistics show young single moms live near the poverty level. If young men have to pay child support, it can take money out of their check that would otherwise be available to save. I have paid over $70,000 in child support from my early twenties into my late thirties.

Young people that get married need to make sure they stay married because divorce can be very costly. It has been reported to be one of the most expensive events in a person's lifetime, especially if children are involved. Additionally, people should remain healthy. Medical bills can be very costly as well if a person is unhealthy in their lifetime with the biggest portion of the expense occurring after 60 years old because of the cost of medication and frequent visits to the doctor's office and/or hospital. These are some of the things young people should keep in the forefront of their mind as they plan to secure their financial future.

"Understand what is in and out of your control before spending lavishly because money can become a limited resource and it should be treated as such when you receive it."

Kevin Powell (KP)

"It is better to have and not need, than to need and not have." Anonymous

CHAPTER ONE

The Reality about Money: Saving and Spending

*"If you would know the value of money, go try to borrow
some; for he that goes a-borrowing goes a-sorrowing."*
Ben Franklin

Consumer debt is enormous. The economic state of the
nation and world is an indication that directly correlates with
consumers' obsession with spending. The United States of
America (USA) National Debt is $15 trillion dollars, the USA
Federal Budget Deficit is $1.3 trillion, and the USA Federal
spending is $3.6 trillion. Overspending could be contributed to
living in a consumer driven society.

When you hear stimulate the economy, it is intended
for consumers to spend more money. It could be money we
have saved or future earnings. When people do not have
money they typically use their credit card, borrow the money
from someone. The media has a vested interest in prodding
consumers (citizens) to spend. They profit from
advertisements. As a result of consumer spending, the USA

1

has the largest gross domestic product GDP in the world. Consumer spending accounts for 70% of economic activity in the USA.

Consumers have more power than they think. They have spending and saving power. They have the power to influence markets, politics, regulations, and trends. Many companies would not exist if citizens changed their spending habits. If citizens collectively understood their power, collectively we would eliminate most of the world's indebtedness and our own. Currently, we are living and witnessing a vicious cycle of spending and borrowing at an alarming rate, the highest level in America's history.

Consumers are driven to buy and then they are trapped in the web of debt. I hate to use the analogy but it is like consumers are being lead like livestock to the feeding area. Out of all of the things we consume we technically do not own any of it. The same thing applies to the money we earn and invest; we do not own any of it. If you fail to pay the taxes on your property, the county or municipality may put a lien on it and then sell it. If you miss a couple of house or car payments, the banks threaten to foreclose or repossess it. Your house could catch fire or a burglar could break in and clean your house out. If we lose or gain weight, we buy new clothes and then donate or throw away the old clothes.

The need to shop uncontrollably is all an illusion driven by desires and subtle pressures in our society. Once wanting ceases, happiness starts to develop. Pleasure and pain are dual opposites, when we get excited about purchasing items at some point it loses its initial luster and then we may ask ourselves what made me want this and what was I thinking. Consuming provides short-term gratification that can lead to long-term pain. If you are not careful, when you buy items you could be serving your ego to satisfy an emotional desire.

A large portion of the USA population mismanages their money. They get inundated with sales ads and overzealous with spending; eventually they struggle to get ahead financially. As a country, we cannot seem to understand the concept of saving enough money over time to make purchases with cash. Some would say, we live in a society that want things *"now and we mean right now."* In others words, we want instant gratification; we do not want to wait for it. We think if we wait for it, it may not have the same gratifying feeling that we could obtain in the moment of craving. Our impulsive spending habit is mind boggling and it has to be readjusted sooner than later to create financial stability.

What habits are we teaching our children? Whether habits are good or bad those habits have a tendency to stick with children for life. Therefore, parents have to be more responsible for teaching their children about saving and budgeting. Adults without children are equally responsible and should find time to mentor children and teach them about money management. As a nation, everyone has to assume responsibility and hold each other accountable. We have to step back and look at the big financial picture; reprioritize and reassess our saving versus spending ratio, so we can be better stewards of our hard earned cash.

Long-term effect of debt

Debt causes anxiety, stress and hinder personal, professional, and spiritual growth, which could be related to the over utilization of antidepressants and painkillers in our country. In 2008, the antidepressant market generated over $10 billion dollars in sales, which does not include generic mediations and psychotropic medications. When you learn the true value of money, you realize it could become a limited resource; especially if a life event occurs that reduces income, i.e. job layoff, a decrease in investment portfolio value, or continued decrease in the value of dollar. Managing and watching how much you are actually paying out of pocket for living expenses and extravagant shopping requires effort. Debt can find and plague the most well intended person, a person that earns a lot or a little amount of money. Debt is indiscriminate. To reduce and erase debt, it starts with paying down debt and saving more money from every pay check and taking minimal financial risks. Money should always be treated like a limited resource and a gift from God. Many things can drain a savings account, i.e. medical bills, prescription drugs, serious accident, job loss or a crash in the stock market similar to 2008.

The United States, its citizens, and the global economy are experiencing financial challenges and on the verge of experiencing perpetual recession. The United States credit rating has been affected and many citizens are seeing their credit rating plummet because of the high rate of foreclosures and unemployment. There were over one million homes foreclosed in 2011. Unemployment is hovering near 9% for the general population. Some critics say it is higher for different segments of the population.

For real time economic data see:
http://www.usdebtclock.org

The Reality about Money: Saving and Spending

Given the economic challenges our country is facing there is an opportunity to create a platform to teach our children about money management, banking, credit cards, credit scores, interest rates, mortgages, investments and savings to help individuals circumvent future financial calamities. In a global economy all countries are linked together; as a result, they are in the same predicament. Money and banking are part of America's fabric. Banking is an established institution that people in the United States of America cannot get around when they become adults. People cannot get around money either because we need it to function in society. We do not need it to live but it has been made to be a necessity. That is why it is necessary to learn about it and save it.

It amazes me and other people that are concerned about financial literacy that more financial programs and curriculums do not exist to teach young people how to properly manage money before they become adults. Learning about money management is as important as learning about math, science, reading, and healthy living. If children can progressively learn those subjects they can learn about banking and investing as well. Children are taught to identify money, add and subtract money, but education is lacking on how to manage it. The nation's debt crisis is an effect of national financial illiteracy. You would think there would be an outcry by national, state, and local leaders that something needs to be done to stymie the out of control spending.

In the beginning of 2012, President Obama asked Congress to raise the debt ceiling by an additional 1.2 trillion dollars. The opposite action would have been better and it would have sent a message to the country that it is important to reduce debt and credit limits. It is better to be financially responsible by eliminating debt and expenditures than to continue increasing the line of credit to continue to overspend.

Daily news reports, non-profit and for-profit organizations have an opportunity to warn adults of the harmful effects of overspending. There are ads for the harmful effects of smoking and contracting STDs. There are ads about preventing unwanted pregnancy. Accumulating debt ranks right up there with those concerns. If the government regulates tobacco companies to warn teens and adults about tobacco, why not require banks to advertise a public announcement about debt. The message should be clear to children and parents that learning about money and banking are important. Children should start learning about money and banking at a young age and develop good money habits. As adults they will be able to stay the course and in a safe harbor from the sharks waiting to take advantage of their ignorance about money and banking. Parents have to protect and take care of their children by sharing their wisdom as soon as possible. Parents have to adopt the mindset that they are protecting their children like eagles protect their young for long-term survival. Otherwise the children are conditioned to consume and to feel the need to make spurt of the moment buying decisions when they should be saving.

The ego is partly responsible for consumers buying more than they need. The ego can lead us to great misery, stress and pain. The ego is just another word for desire. That desire can be deeply embedded in our psychology and constructed concepts depending on the metal conditioning to budget. Children can be conditioned to spend excessively during periods of sadness or happiness, instead of spending when they need the item the most. Our ancestors believed in consuming only out of necessity. They were focused on protecting the land and nature. That philosophy should be reconsidered before we face another global economic meltdown and greater financial catastrophe. It all boils down to increasing financial literacy and saving more cash.

How hard could it be to teach children in their formative years (grade school) about money? There should be a standardize test at the end of the year on money principles and basics banking. There are some schools that teach children about money and they are an exception to the majority of schools in the country. To our country humiliation, there are people in the world that prefer to perpetuate the conservative and discriminative tradition of haves and have not, rich and poor and superiority and inferiority. Therefore, if all children learn about money it levels the playing field and dispels the illusion that people are inherently better than others. Financial equality is unacceptable to some despite inequality being disharmonious and unjustifiable. Our county and the world would benefit from the USA having a money management curriculum or more programs dedicated to training youth. To develop a stronger nation, our children need more formal money management and career focus programs to teach them how to save, spend and invest, to prevent future economic crises or recessions. Too often our children are clueless about what career path to pursue and how to manage their money when they finally select a career path.

How long would it take to save a year or a half of a year annual salary if you make that a goal?

If parents and schools do not teach children about banking who will? If parents do not train their children or seek proper training, they leave their children vulnerable to dishonest people resembling con artists and snake oil salesmen, and to learning through trial and error. Parents can teach their children as best as they can but at the end of the day they need formal guidance and structure. In some cases when parents teach their children about money, it's like the blind leading the blind down the same dark and muddy path of financial trouble but a least a best effort should be attempted. If nothing more, the parent should consistently encourage their child(ren) to save.

The majority of parents know as much about the banking industry and finances as their fore parents, which is not that much when you consider the constant evolution of banking and investing. Parents know how to go to work to make money and then how to spend it. Few parents know how to save and invest it.

The statistics speak for themselves; the average single family has a negative savings. To improve the national financial literacy level, school systems should strongly consider implementing a program or curriculum that teaches financial literacy to stave off future personal and national economic crises. The questions then becomes how authentic and relevant is the information that is going to be taught in the school system that will be applicable in the real world as it continues to change at a rapid pace. Will the information be good enough for the time we live in? Will it be beneficial in the present and future? I would say yes, if we learn at least the basics, which are to save and live below our monthly income.

Learning about the proper management of money and the banking industry is important for students to learn because there is no way they can avoid using a bank as adults. The necessity to go to a bank is like the necessity to breathe air or drink water to stay hydrated. Equally important is the need to learn about the value of money and when to apply limitation on money. Who knows the future value of a dollar? Gold is steadily rising as the American currency fluctuates. The strength of money could erode because of inflation or stronger currency against the dollar in other countries such as the Chinese Yuan.

Furthermore, it is important for children to develop good money skills and acumen because they may want to exchange United States money for a stronger currency and save it until they are older adults or trade it at some point to earn more. Additionally, instead of saving U.S. cash, a person may decide to buy gold or precious metals to secure or protect (hedge) their savings.

Americans are challenged and limited in their knowledge about money. They have learned from their socioeconomic plight and environment in which they socialize. Unfortunately too many people learn the hard way by becoming a victim of financial calamities which often times takes years to recover from which could seem like a lifetime.

There are success stories of children saving and investing at an early age. They learned the value of money and they used it wisely. If people do not know what it takes to protect their financial interest and how to save for the sake of saving, they are vulnerable to predators in the business and financial industries.

There are many material things and people in this world clamoring for your money. Learning about how to earn, preserve, and spend money is crucial to our livelihood. There are people that profit from our lack of financial knowledge and banks just happens to be one of them because they operate credit card companies, finance companies, mortgage companies, and student loan companies.

Save Cash

Banks are constantly looking for ways to increase their profits; after all, they are a for-profit entity and publicly traded on the stock market. For an example in 2011, checking account fees were averaging about $50 a year, which is double what was paid in 2010. The minimum amount to keep in a checking account has doubled, according to a 2011 Checking Account Survey. Banks are charging more for overdraft fees, wire transfers, and paper statements. Free checking accounts have decreased and continue to do so. Monthly maintenance fees have increased. Because of recent changes in banking regulations that caused banks to lose a substantial amount of revenue to the tune of $20 billion, banks have to earn between $85-$115 per account, which will come in the hidden fees and extra charges. In 2011 because of consumer push back on debit card fees, top banks decided not to go forward with implementing no policies that would charge customers debit fees.

Americans have to keep a closer eye on bank fees. If fees continue increasing, which they will, we should ask ourselves, what can we do differently to manage banking fees and make sure we are getting the full banking services that meet our needs instead of the banks dictating to us what we should accept. You may decide to stick with your bank in the end, but you may well decide to move all your money to a credit union with fewer fees and similar services.

Banks loan money deposited and charges us a premium to borrow it. Ironically, they cannot give you the same return on your money that they are charging you in loan interest rates. If you go to take out a personal loan the interest rate will be between 4-7% and in some cases higher, depending on your credit. Unfortunately, they will not pay you 4-7% interest on the money you deposit in their bank. That is the imbalance Americans are passively living with. We can make excuses for banks and make justification all day long for them being a business. The reality is they have a business to run and they have to charge fees that will help offset their expenses which include salaries. We could debate whether they are doing us a favor by holding our money. Are they really doing us a service when you consider the .08% to 1% they offer us in interest payments for accounts with $25,000 or more? To me that is a win-loss situation and consumers are on the losing end. They operate to loan money for businesses, homes, land, recreational items and automobiles.

According to 2011 banking reports posted online, interest bearing checking accounts continues to become less attractive for account holders. Yields were down for the fifth consecutive year dating back to 2006-2011, falling 2 basis points to an all-time low of 0.08 percent. Even as yields fell, fees rose. The average monthly maintenance fee for an interest-bearing checking account jumped 8.5 percent, from $13.05 to $14.05. Like ATM fees, overdraft fees tend to rise at or near the rate of inflation, and this year is no exception. The average nonsufficient funds, or NSF, fee rose 1 percent, from $30.47 last year to a record $30.83 this year.

We are taught to go with the flow and accept what society dictates. We are taught to deal with it because that is what the market will bear. There are limited options available to be able to avoid banks completely, which is why it is important for children to learn about banking and financing at a very young age.

Electronic deposits and electronic debits automatic payment are separating us from our money. Today we rarely touch and feel cash to connect with it, to be familiar with its texture and get in the habit of using it; instead, we use plastic cards, wire transfers or electronic transmissions. Consequently, we are devaluing money and under appreciating its true value and benefit to our overall health and livelihood. Because life is lived at a fast pace, it becomes a matter of convenience to have our payroll check directly deposited, set bills up on auto-pay and to swipe a debit card.

If a local or national power grid were to fail or if a major disaster occurs that knocks out our banking computer system, how would we make transactions or get money in that time of a crisis? We have to make it a habit to have cash on hand to get used to having it around to accumulate it.

The classroom setting

Money Management could very well be a course or two in school. It could consist of learning money terminology, bank terminology, interest equations for saving long term, and case studies. There could be advance classes offered and taught by a math or a finance teacher. Students could learn about trading stocks and bonds, buying and selling commodities, investing in annuities, researching and selecting investment vehicles, managing an investment portfolio and analyzing rates of returns on real estate investments. Learning about money in the classroom can be limitless and only limited by the knowledge of the teacher and school system.

Teaching children financial literacy could develop future generations to avoid personal debt and future global financial crises. Children would be able to make better financial decisions and manage their financial transactions. If more people knew about economics and finance, they would be able to hold themselves, businesses and governments more accountable for financial decisions.

What are the reluctances to teaching children about money management? Where does the breakdown in financial communication cease and begin in our school system? Why adults do not know more than they do about managing the money they earn or that they may be giving? Why are financial illiterate parents left with the burden to teach their children about money? The conversation starts with the community and elected officials. The cycle of financial illiteracy has been perpetuated for too many generations. The cycle has to stop sooner than later and it has to start with teaching our young people. As it is today in the year 2012, children are at the mercy of their parents for financial literacy. Families and society has to set up and show more concern for raising the stakes of financial literacy for our children's sake.

Parents, community leaders, policy makers and all businesses can be held accountable for financial literacy. Students need to learn how to finance college or technical school. Otherwise, they will take out loans with an obligation to pay back or they could work and save their money to pay for college. Instead of borrowing money, the money they earn and save can go towards tuition, living expenses and books.

Our children have great potential to understand money, they our future in the words in the song by the late Whitney Houston, *"teach them well and let them lead the way."* Americans wonder why we are in debt to China and Saudi Arabia. It is obvious to observers that the USA is not preparing enough of their children for a prosperous economic future. Why should only a few people know about finances and the monetary system? Is there an unwritten law in the constitution? If so, it should be amended and a new bill should be introduced and signed into law that every public school across our nation will teach financial education in grade school.

If the history of money is taught, there is hope that it would hold their attention because of the new information they will discover and the appetite children have for money. Children like talking about money. Children may ask questions about money out of their natural curiosity about things. At a young age, children learn that money is for spending and that they need to earn plenty of it so they can buy items. Lessons about saving money should be fixed in their mind and seen as a path to financial security.

Think for a few seconds and ask yourself is it necessary to borrow money for everything you want if you have an opportunity to save for it weeks, months or years in advance? It is not necessary to purchase an expensive wedding ring, vacation house or the largest flat screen television in the neighborhood. While we are accumulating all these things, we end up saving less money and spending less time with our family and more time on the job to repay the money we owe.

Parents have to start teaching their children to save and reinforce it by holding back immediate gratifications, which teaches discipline and the need to save money per pay check. A "do as I say and as I do" philosophy is a great principle to live by. Recently my youngest daughter wanted a princess vanity set that cost $74.99. I shared with her when dad receives two separate checks we will purchase it. Initially, she was not satisfied with my decision because of her desire to satisfy her immediate wish. As an adult she will appreciate those types of lessons. It teaches patience and discipline. We hope she will appreciate the item more and learn to control her impulsive urges. To reinforce the behavior I shared the strategy with my wife and she completely supported it which is necessary if the child is going to learn how to save. My best efforts to train my daughter would not take hold if my wife gave into my daughter's insatiable desire for consumption. Because we waited until we had saved the money for the vanity, we were able to get it online for $47.99 instead paying the retail price of $74.99. Ultimately, we saved considerably. If we had bought it when she first asked for it and paid for it using our credit card, we would have paid interest for the item and we would have paid more money for the item. Therefore, we saved by not paying interest to a credit card company and we kept money in our pocket. Many times it pays to be patient and to save money over a period of time to get what we need. Being patient can help build contentment and wealth in the long run.

CHAPTER TWO

Learn the Value of Money and Start Saving

Set your lifestyle below your earned income because income can always go away and you do not want to be effected by not having it for a period of time. KP

Dealing with banks can be a major new experience for young adults once they become 18 years old. Particularly for college students that go off to college because they are away from the watchful eyes of adult supervision. Therefore, they have to put in action the lessons they have been taught about managing money. Many children willingly accept the responsibility and look forward to independent living. As a young adult in college with no parents to supervise them, they are left to make their own decisions. They have some basic financial needs while on campus but not much.

If a child is versed in saving and managing money at an early age they stand to benefit when they are in college. The money they saved can supplement the money their parents are able to give them. There will be some cases when the parents are unable to send money to them. Therefore, the money the child worked and earned growing up will be valuable in college. Additionally, they will be in a better financial position than the child that did not have the lessons about money growing up.

The notion of saving as early and as often as possible is vital to developing a sound financial grounding. It is never too early to start saving and training children to save. Parents can start saving for the child before the child is born. Bridal showers can become a money shower and a great event to announce the start of a college fund for the child for friends and family to contribute towards.

I remember going to college and receiving $20-40 dollars a week from my grandma and parents. I was very appreciative of the money they sent me and I love them dearly for it. I was dependent on them sending money. If they did not send money timely, I had to patiently wait until they did. Looking back on it, I was too dependent on them. It is a tough living when someone else has to provide for you when you are an adult.

The money they eventually sent was spent washing clothes and purchasing a few items for evening snacks to share with friends. If I had been one of the children taught to save I would not have had to depend on my parents' financial support. If I had had been taught the value of money and how to manage as a youth, I would have saved a portion of all of my earnings and money collected during special occasions and from part-time jobs.

We can learn lessons from nature like animals and insects. For example, squirrels store nuts for the winter and ants save food for a later time as well. They realize a time will come when they will need the food they have stored. It is impossible to watch and know how much money your neighbor is stashing away because saving money is personal and confidential information. Rarely do people share how much they save monthly or annually. Therefore, saving money has to become an individual decision and personal commitment.

Obtaining financial literacy as a young child has many benefits. Children could learn about investing, compounding interest, buying and selling stocks and bonds and living off the compounding interest the investments are generating. I read an article recently in the USA today that Mitt Romney a presidential candidate was paying income taxes based only on the interest he was earning from his investments. In other words, his income was the interest from his investments. He was living off his investments, which is the reason he was only paying an effective rate of 15% of taxes. More people can do that too, if they learn about money and start saving and investing at an early age.

At the age of 18 you can take money out of your trust fund, college fund, or CD that your parents, grandparents, your loved ones and you contributed to over your childhood. It is highly recommended that children be given donations for college throughout their young life instead of receiving all non-monetary gifts on their birthday, holidays, and for accomplishments.

During holidays and birthdays parents might spend $250-$500. When you total the amount of money spent over a child's young age until they turn 18, it could easily equate to $20,000, ($750x18 years). $20,000 could cover the expense of four years of in-state college tuition depending on the college. If you saved $20,000 and the child does not need the money for school because they might receive a scholarship, the money could remain saved or invested. When feasible the money could be used towards graduate school, a car, a wedding or a home. We have to start rethinking the value of money and think that it is possible and mandatory to hoard it. As Americans we have to become more comfortable with saving large sums of money.

I have heard parents tell their child, "I want to give you something now to play with or to have and for you to know it came from me." That thinking is short term and shallow. If love ones care about the child, saving money for the child's education would be more beneficial for the child in the long run. I would like to think love ones would like to know they are contributing to the child's education. In essence, they are helping them pay for college or giving them a head start in life. Some of the things we buy our children are unnecessary and other things are too lavish. Giving money that will go into a college fund or savings account for the child has more meaning and value. Otherwise, when you buy gifts you are making others rich that are already wealthy. When was the last time you saw a major retailer that you shop at make a large donation to your community, school, or college? If you are going to spend money with retailers and grocery stores, I highly recommend being a member of *Upromise*. *Upromise* helps parents save money for college when parents and love ones shop with vendors that support *Upromise*. As a member of *Upromise*, a percentage of the money you spend with companies that support *Upromise* goes into a savings account to help pay for college.

Learn the Value of Money and Start Saving

Many top retailers generate tens and hundreds of billions of dollars annually in revenue from people that spend fanatically and needlessly. Cutting back on spending just a little adds money to the savings pile at the end of the month. Do the math and talk to a financial planner to see how much money you would need to save monthly or annually to fund a college education. You will quickly learn why learning about money and teaching children about money is vitally important.

Unbeknown to college students banks are on college campuses in sheep clothing and lurking as wolves in disguise. Sadly for many students, banks are on campus as credit card solicitors. This may be the first time ever dealing with a banking representative as well being faced with a monumental financial decision that could haunt them for a life time if they accept their offer to get a credit card.

I first encountered credit card solicitors when I was 18 at my alma mater in the student union (popular location) in front of the bookstore and near student mailboxes. They had a table strategically placed in the student union to encounter the most students. The student union was the most trafficked spot because people went to get a drink or snack from the bookstore or get their mail for the day. Credit card solicitors select prime location on college campuses across the country. Fortunately, some college campuses restrict and prohibit credit card companies from soliciting students. More colleges should revisit their campus solicitation policy and adopt a stricter non-solicitation policy given the havoc credit cards create in young people lives. Students are in school getting an education. If students are solicited, they should be required to have their parents co-sign the application if the students have a student status.

A studied conducted U.S. Public Interest Research Group showed that two out of three students have at least one credit card and at least 76% of students stop at the credit card companies table to look at credit card offers. 80% of students said they receive mail from credit card companies at an average rate of almost five offers a month.

In my personal experience and what has been reported by researchers, credit card companies give away cheap trinkets like water bottles and tee shirts to entice students. Their objective is to get students to sign up for a credit card. Who knows how many lives have been destroyed by marketing strategies and tactics used in an environment that students and parents considered safe zones; not realizing when we send our children to college they could be in a danger zone. Countless students have fallen prey to the smiling faces and cordial handshakes of credit card representatives. Most students do not realize what they are getting themselves into until years later when they remember their first encounter with a young person about their age who solicited them to sign up for a credit card.

How much money do the colleges receive for allowing banks to solicit to students? What incentives do employees of banks receive when they sign people up for a credit card? I realize they are doing their job as representatives of the credit card company and that is their sole reason for doing it but are they consciously aware of what they are doing to a person's life when the person is not astute about finances and money management? It could takes years before a person realizes they have a bad habit of using credit cards and it takes even longer to stop using them and to pay off the debt.

We have to be careful what we become dependent on. A better use for banks on the college campus would be for them to partner with colleges to offer a course in money management and banking. Then allow students the opportunity to decide to sign up for a credit card after they have completed the course or training class. In that class, scenarios and real stories should be shared with students about the number of people in debt and unable to pay their credit card bills. It should discuss the ramification for not paying the balance and the impact of paying late. When students sign on the dotted line their world changes and their life will never be the same. They are forced into responsible adulthood instantaneously without them even knowing it. Ideally, colleges should have a curriculum and require students to take courses that teach financial literacy before they can graduate to prepare them for living and working in society.

Independence from credit cards is much better than being dependent on them. Hence Independence Day and the desire of the founding Fathers of the United States of America to gain their independence from Great Britain to become a sovereign nation. The U.S.A. was required to pay taxes and repay loans to Great Britain to gain independence. The U.S.A. borrowed money to establish the U.S.A. Later in the deal, they were tired of having to pay the British government a portion of their wages. The British government likes banks, raised fees and prices of goods as much as they wanted. They realized they could raise rates and prices regardless of how the colonial settlers felt about it, which is similar to banks and credit companies today. The entities controlling the money and terms of the loan have the power to do as they please unless there is tight regulation by the government. Banks can raise fees and interest when they find it suitable to meet their needs.

"Life, Liberty and the Pursuit of Happiness"
United States of America Declaration of Independence

It takes a strong will, discipline and knowledge about money to live a life independent of banks. Assistance from a financial planner can be beneficial; I highly recommend working with one early in your career. The reason it is difficult to be financially independent is because you feel like you can buy what you want instantly even if you do not have the cash on hand by using a credit card. Subsequently, people start to add their credit card line into their income, which should be avoided. Once you become overextend or obligated to repay money, you become the slave and not the master. Eventually, the items you buy and the lender you borrowed money from control you because you are forced to generate enough money to pay back the money you borrowed. It can be an emotionally challenging and an unnecessary nightmare.

When I received my first credit card I immediately felt like I aged a few years. It was like having more power, ego, and vitality. I could spend at will. I became an adult overnight. My consuming options immediately expanded and I had purchasing options never before available because in times past I had to wait for funds or save money. The first few things I bought were a pair of jeans, a sweater, and shoes. I was making plans to wear the outfit to a popular college basketball game (NCCU vs NC A&T at the Greensboro Coliseum) and I wanted to look good. The card inflated my ego and false sense of self-worth. Although the credit line was between $500 and $700 dollars, I never should have had it because I did not have a job to pay the full credit limit if I had spent up to the limit. The money my parents sent eventually went towards paying the balance until I received a refund from student loan to pay the full balance due, which was money I still eventually had to repay.

According to a 2009 study done by college lender Sallie Mae, 92% of college students with credit cards used their credit cards to obtain textbooks, school supplies, and pay for tuition which is up from 85% in 2008. Credit card utilization among college students is steadily increasing. "84% of undergraduates had at least one credit card, up from 76% in 2004. On average, students have 4.6 credit cards, and half of college students had four or more cards. The average (mean) balance grew to $3,173, higher than any of the previous studies. Median debt grew from 2004's $946 to $1,645 in

2009. The higher the grade level, the more heavily students used their credit cards, with seniors graduating with an average credit card debt of more than $4,100, up from about $2,900 in 2004. The study found that freshmen carried a median debt of $939; nearly triple the $373 in 2004. Only 15% of freshmen had a zero credit card balance, a dramatic drop from 69% in the 2004 study. 60% experienced surprise at how high their balance had reached, and 40% said they have charged items knowing they did not have the money to pay the bill. Only 17% said they regularly paid off all cards each month, and another 1% had parents, a spouse, or other family members paying the bill. The remaining 82% carried balances and thus incurred finance charges each month. 84% of undergraduates indicated they needed more education on financial management topics. In fact, 64% would have liked to receive information in high school and 40% as college freshmen."

Sallie Mae's study is indicative that many college students are victims of the same credit card schemes year after year. It is for these reason, colleges should not permit credit card companies to solicit to students unless they offer a credit card education program. To help students, colleges should educate them about being financially responsible. Colleges could consider inviting banks onto campus to educate students about the costs associated with credit cards and the appropriate usage to prevent overindulgence that leads to being unable to pay the full balance or missing payments.

During my college days or in my adult life I have not witnessed or heard of banks volunteering to educate college students or the local community about money management. There are no excuses for them not reaching out to colleges and communities to provide training and money management tips. There are usually many bank branches in a city near a college. They could host events to educate the community in which they do business. Most bankers live in the surrounding community where they work; participation in community events should be easy. They spend millions to market to the community their loan services for personal and business usage. Community leaders should invite bankers to participate in and sponsor community based financial educational seminars. Local banks should be considered to offer scholarships and stipends to high school and college students. Additionally, they could be asked to pay a stipend to a teacher to teach money management full-time or part-time. Participation from local banks would increase the financial literacy of the people they serve in the community. Then that community would be a more educated consumer base that would understand money management and the proper reasons for obtaining and using a credit card or loan.

Colleges, banks, community leaders, parents, and youths can create partnerships. To make it a reality will require leadership, authenticity, collaboration, dedication, creativity, innovation and support from the community.

CHAPTER THREE

Credit Cards

"Put money in thy pocket." William Shakespeare

Having a large credit line and living on credit cards is a false sense of wealth and security. If you are making only the minimum monthly payment on credit cards, that means you are living above your income and that you have over spent. When you pay less than the full balance on the credit card, you are setting yourself up for high interest charges that could lead to unmanageable debt. As consumers we have to rethink our purchasing decisions. It is wise to remove thoughts of purchasing if it puts you at risk of credit card debt and not being able to save.

As parents we have to be responsible for the financial education of our children. We can no longer allow our children to walk into financial darkest feeling around for the light searching for the right path because life's lessons can be difficult. To some it can be devastating and traumatic. Recovery from bad financial decisions is possible. However, why should our children be subject to financial hardship, which could set them back for years? To have our children go

35

through a harsh recovery period due to lack of knowledge on their part and improper training on our part is amoral and unfair to our children. As parents we should be embarrassed to contribute to the process of financial struggle and stand up to provide them with proper training to make wise money management decisions as adults.

Traditionally, our way of living and the vices that exist drive us down the road of financial blunder. Financial challenges sometimes can lead to criminal activity. Furthermore, there are individuals, businesses and smooth talkers waiting to seize and feast on individual's financial illiteracy and predicament. Society is full of money traps and trappers. Do not be fooled by the inducements and special offers thrown at you through mass media, i.e. television, radio, billboards, and mobile applications. This is a money hungry culture driven by profits and greed to provide for someone else's lavish lifestyle.

There are businesses that want us to consume until we cannot consume anymore or until we are dead broke. Greed does not have a heart or soul. Consumerism is a large magnet pulling at our money. For example, after you have bought enough for yourself businesses want you to buy for your family and friends, i.e. holidays, special occasions. If that is not enough, the subtle pressure is placed on us to buy a large house with big walk-in closets to put excessive and expensive clothes and shoes.

There are some people that have clothes in their closets with price tags still on them and shoes in boxes that they have never worn. Some people spend like the money stream is infinite and it will never run out. That is our conditioned mentality. It is as if we are trying to satisfy an unidentifiable subconscious craving that is inflamed by desire and stoked by the media and our ego. Media can have a profound effect on our ego and buy decisions if we are not cautious. Have you noticed every public place you go has music and/or television? We cannot get away from constant bombardment of subliminal messaging that push our buttons to crave more despite our intuitive instinct to turn off the commercials and save our hard earned money that is becoming harder to come by.

Recently, I read an article that a major drug company was going to freeze salaries for most of their employees. To me that is incomprehensible when companies are making record profits since 2009 and CEOs are earning millions of dollars. During a recession, companies feel employees should be happy to be working despite them earning record profits. That tells me that some companies devalue employees.

Inflation and the cost of goods and services will continue to increase while wages stay the same is appalling and it should be unacceptable. The main theme I am trying to draw out is that saving is critical going forward in the new era of a unified global monetary system. More businesses are continuing to report that they will be reducing severance packages and health benefits after employees get laid-off.

Typically, when we muster the will that stops us from purchasing, there is still a nagging thought process that we should be purchasing. We have to constantly fight the invisible and visible forces that get in our heads when we know we do not have the money. Resist the urge and isolate the ego. When we give in and turn to spending and using credit cards we stand the chance of losing the war against managing and saving our money.

Credit cards should not be used to make impulsive or frivolous purchases. Credit cards should be used in an emergency situation only. If credit cards are used in a non-emergency the money should be available to pay the balance in full when the bill arrives. Cash should be used instead of credit cards because using cash helps regulate our spending. Our financial inhibitions are drastically lowered when we have several credit cards in our wallet. People have a tendency to spend less when they have cash in their wallets instead of credit cards because we connect the money leaving our hand with it no longer being in our possession. It has a psychological effect on our behavior when we see money leaving our hand that gives us pause when shopping and causes us to think multiple times about spending it. If we use credit cards we generally spend more and make larger purchases.

Too many small purchases can add up over time and can grow into a pile of debt and lost money. When we use cash we are more aware of our spending limitations and the price we are paying. We mentally calculate and track the number of items we are purchasing when we use cash. We keep our guards up when cashed is used. Otherwise when using credit cards it is easy to lose track of spending, especially if we have a large credit limit. As an example, when we know the credit limit is small we shop less, which is similar to having a certain amount of cash on hand to spend. With credit cards people have a tendency to over spend because of the temptation to purchase and pay later. It may be wise to rethink and reprioritize our credit card versus cash on hand ratio and to think about all of the costs associated with using a credit card, i.e. annual fees, interest rate, and any extra charges for cash advancements or overdue payments.

We are entering into an era of ultimate consumerism perpetual household debt unless we stop and think about cash money in a different light. Cash is our friend but debt and credit can be our worst enemy if we are not vigilant and on top of it. Try not to be deluded by the puppets on commercials that portray that everything is wonderful and glamorous when using credit cards. It is a fallacy and seduction. The world of banking and finance is transitioning at a rapid speed from cash to plastic and from PC to mobile applications to purchase goods and services. Why does a check card have to have a credit card company's logo on it? Indirect messages are ever present so we can get comfortable using credit cards for routine shopping and for it to become second nature. We are known to be creatures of habit. Credit cards are for the 1% not the 99% of the U.S. population. In the early 1980's the banking industry was deregulated which allowed banks to market credit cards to the remaining 99% of society. It was an opportunity for banks and major investors to profit from the interest generated from consumer debt and profit from a larger pool of Americans that had decent credit and could qualify for credit cards, which was later duplicated with housing deregulation and predatory lending.

Technically, the wealthy do not need credit cards. Instead they carry them as a matter of convenience. If more consumers saved, they would not need credit cards either, which would be to their own benefits in the long run to help establish personal wealth.

To make it more convenient for impulsive spenders, businesses are highly focused and determined to make the shopping experience easy and thoughtless. Mobile commerce or "m-commerce" is the new buzz word among businesses.

M-commerce is becoming popularized through downloading smart phone applications and the iPad is the number one device used followed by Android "apps store or Google Play" as the platform to download applications onto smart phones. Over time m-commerce will have 24/7 access to our mobile wallet to buy items, make payments, track our spending and every move we make to direct us toward sales, discounts and special offers from the retailers where we like to shop or to their affiliates. Major companies large and small are rushing to capture the market and consumer's dollars. Many top companies have already launched their telecommunication software platforms. The software platforms that companies are teaming up to create with the banking industry will be larger and more comprehensive than anything we have ever seen in mobile communication, mobile technology or mobile banking.

The benefit to the businesses is their credit card fees will be reduced significantly, so they will pay less money in transaction fees to their credit card host, which means more revenue for them. Business will be able to send consumers advertisement via their smart phone. Mobile wallet and other mobile applications will revolutionize the online shopping and checkout process because it will store credit card and banking information, which has the potential to nudge us to spend more than we would normally spend. In order for Americans to save more money to build generational wealth, they will need to remain focus on saving and budgeting.

Save Cash

Card Services
Post Office Box ████

March 27, 2012

KEVIN D POWELL

Dear KEVIN D POWELL:

Re: Account ending in ████

As you requested on March 27, 2012, we closed your above-referenced credit card account.

Please destroy all credit cards and SUPERCHECKS™. When the account was closed, any links for Overdraft Protection were also canceled. If there is a balance on the account, you will continue to receive your monthly billing statements.

If you have authorized any companies to charge your account for membership fees or ongoing services, please contact them directly to arrange an alternate method of payment.

We are sorry that you decided to close your ████████ credit card account and hope that you will give us the opportunity to serve you again in the future.

If you have questions, please call us at 1-800-████████. Our representatives are here to assist you 24 hours a day, 7 days a week.

████████ Card Services

43

CHAPTER FOUR

Consumerism and Materialism

Strongly consider getting a financial planner to help chart your financial course.

In 2011 U.S. mobile commerce sales exceeded $5.3 billion, up 83% over 2010. A mobile commerce research firm projects that mobile commerce usage will grow by 600% to 490 million people worldwide by 2014. That's more than the U.S.A. population, which has a population close to 313 million as of December 2011.

At the beginning of 2011, First Data, an Atlanta, GA company that handles payment processing and verification, asked people how long would it take for mobile phone transaction to surpass credit card transactions, most expected 10 years. Now, it's closer to three to four years because of the younger generation's passion for mobile phones and their quick adaptability to mobile shopping. Mobile commerce is spawning new technology companies and growing existing companies into major players in the mobile commerce space. Square is one of those new software companies. Since their launch in October 2011, they have seen a double amount of

44

payment processed every quarter, and the company is on pace to process $2 billion in payments annually, which is more than the Gross Domestic Product (GDP) = *{the market value of all final goods and services from a nation in a given year}* of some countries. Another new startup is Isis *which also is translated into Aset in Ancient Egypt parlance means wisdom.* According to *Isis'* official "consumers carry up to 800 million credit cards between them (an average of 2.6 card per U.S. citizen), and when you put that together with the connectivity of the mobile phone, there's potential to really change the way consumers shop, pay, and save on a cultural scale." Isis is planning to build in some opportunities for business to be able to target consumers with relevant offers and deals based on past purchases. How much wisdom or inside information do companies need to have about our shopping habits before it borders on invading privacy and confidentiality?

A financial planner friend of mine commented that, "In the last 20 years the society has been a consumer based society. The ramifications of being a consumer based society are not good for the overall health of the global economy and our personal and household finances." The current economic crisis that officially began in 2008 has not fully recovered as of 2nd quarter 2012. Strongly consider getting a financial planner to help chart your financial course and stick with your budget. Economists and business leaders do not know when the United States economy will fully recover. That's a warning flag to individuals to create a budget and stick to it because no job is secure. With a 66% consumer based society, that means most people are not saving money, which makes the economy more vulnerable and leads to a negative savings rate. Our nation's savings rate is considerably low compared to other countries.

According to a friend that's a credit counselor and one that is a financial planner, our society dictates what we should consume even though our purchase may not have any real meaning or intrinsic value to us. Both financial experts feel that using a credit for non-emergency situations is psychological dependence. Discipline and wisdom are required if we are going to have a credit card for emergencies. The challenge with possessing them is we are programed by consumerism, materialism, and capitalism to want instant gratification. Even as adults, we want it now not over a series of paychecks. Instead, we buy in the moment or when the thought hits us to our detriment.

As I was trying to stay afloat in business, I used my business credit card to pay some business bills. Unfortunately, I maximized out one card and came close to taking several other cards to the limit. Fortunately, the majority of the credit cards companies were willing to work with me under the hardship program with the exception of one. That one company went as far as deducting money from my personal account without my permission to bring my account current because I was two months behind. Like anyone I was upset. That was a new experience for me and it taught me a lesson to never bank with a bank where you have a credit card.

Obsessions can be detrimental to us

We are a nation obsessed with borrowing and spending. A 2011 Christmas Holiday Shopping study showed more than fifty percent of computer tablets shoppers feel happy when they shop. 57% of women versus 51% of men tablet owners say they feel happier shopping. Feeling happy is a transitory emotion that is fleeting. As a society it would benefit us individually and collectively if we connect with our inner core and transcend satisfying our short-term cravings. Then deal with the core of our existence which requires self-examination, a turning inwards and examining and living our core or spiritual values. After reflection and examination we should come to realize that most of our spending habits are impulsive and unplanned which could set us back financially and interrupt our well thought-out and planned budget.

Our desire for more is insatiable and must be self-controlled if we are ever going to be in control of our destiny and establish financial stability. Many people feel guilty after buying items they know they cannot afford. An ancient Kemetic proverb says, *"Know Thyself or Knowledge of Self."* In the process of knowing our self we should seek to understand and accept our financial limitations and live within our means to save for a prosperous future.

In the current state of the world economic affairs, we are leaving our future generation with insurmountable financial obligations and a legacy of spending every dollar we earned which is beyond our immediate comprehension of the impact it will have on them. If we do not train our children properly and set the correct example we are creating carbon copies of habits that will be passed down for countless generations if we are unconscious of our action. The enormity of our nation's debt will be better understood in years to come. However, we are seeing glimpses and hearing theories of what the future will look like. For example, the retirement age is constantly being examined to decide if the age limit needs to be increased and if Medicare and social security will be around for future generations, let alone the baby boomers. The current Medicare payment burden is $81 trillion dollars and social security liability is $15 trillion dollars. To help the country get back on track it will take a new generation of thinkers, planners, and compassionate leaders to be trained as early as grade school. I recognize that it is easier to state than to do. It is worth exploring and then putting a plan in place to implement at least on an individual or household level.

If we have children and save $50 a month for 18 years, you will have saved $10,800 for them without including interest earned if the monthly allowance was deposited into a mutual fund or money market account. So as parents if we were to rethink our spending, we could leave our children a rich inheritance and help them build wealth in their lifetime. When the child becomes an adult and start working, she could save $500 per month for 15 years and stockpile $90,000 without including the interest earned if the money was put in a mutual fund, IRA or Certificate of Deposit (CD). If she combines the $11,000 her parents gave her and the $90,000 she saved on her own, she will have over $100,000 by the time she is 35 years old. Now if that parent teaches her children the same principle, then she would be passing on her wisdom to the next generation to help them look forward to developing financial stability.

We live in an individualistic society. To be a stronger nation we have to rise up together and see ourselves as "One Nation under God Indivisible with Liberty and Justice for All." Then put together our collective effort to build a stronger debt free society and world. The United States of America could be the leading nation that other nations would follow. A formal program should start in the classroom because it is mandatory for all children in the USA to attend school until 18 years old. Students are a captive audience to learn money principles and disciplines. A 2011 survey by the Council of Economic Education showed only 13 states require a personal finance class that teaches high school students some form of financial literacy. For a world leader and super power nation that is a meager number and inexcusable; this statistic highlights the need for greater financial literacy in our classroom and at home.

CHAPTER FIVE

Saving Cash Before and After Purchasing a Vehicle

"Creditors have better memories than debtors."
Benjamin Franklin

Financing a car is similar to having a credit card payment. It is money going out of the wallet instead of being saved to build wealth. To accumulate wealth one of the goals would be to try to purchase a dependable used car with cash instead of making monthly payments because when you make monthly payments on a vehicle you become indebted to your job and the finance company, i.e. bank or credit union. This principle goes back to understanding the need to save cash in order to budget and plan ahead for the future, which gets to the heart of the matter to avoid financing and creating extra expenses. Otherwise, you obligate yourself to working to pay off the debt you have created. Ultimately, falling in the trap that most people that work 8 a.m. to 5 p.m. fall into, which is the reason more people fail to get ahead financially. Instead buyers should strongly consider purchasing a car that is within their means to pay for with cash and one that meets their transportation needs. Those who have a desire to build wealth

51

are searching for ways to save and buy items based on necessity instead of unabated desires.

Be fully aware of your criteria for obtaining a car. It should be economical and appropriate to meet your needs because car trends fluctuate, which could be at your expense if you buy based on flash and trends. For example, vehicles can be popular today and out of style within a few years. Smaller more gas efficient cars make sense but if you are stuck with the larger gas guzzler, you will be disappointed. Cars are like the flavor of the month, especially if you allow your buying decision to be led by popular demand. Recently the trend shifted away from Sport Utility Vehicle (SUVs) because of the increase expenditure of gas prices. SUVs stop being popular when gas prices hit $4.00 per gallon under the Bush Administration; his Administration gave businesses tax incentives for purchasing them not individuals. The more money you spend on gas, the more money the oil companies make and the less money you are able to save. At the time I am writing this book the gas price is in the price range of $3.90 for regular and expected to reach $4 by summer 2012; premium gas is above $4 per gallon. I would like to make the point that it doesn't matter what year it is just know gas prices fluctuates because of supply, demand and inflation and it can go as high as the oil companies (OPEC) dictates. Individuals interested in building wealth should realize powerful politicians could have a vested interest in promoting trends. Elected officials have been known to have a vested interest in big businesses, i.e. oil companies, construction companies, and banks; to them it is about making money, i.e. accumulating wealth.

In some places in the United States gas prices have been as high as $5 per gallon, particularly in California and Nevada. Spending $5 per gallon to fill an 18-25 gallon gas tank will quickly reduce your saving power. The 2000 Ford Excursion had a 44 gallon tank. If you own a SUV, you will not miss many gas stations before you have to stop and refill because the miles per gallon of fuel consumption is in the neighborhood of 11 to 17 miles per gallon depending on city or highway miles. Do the math, the cost adds up quickly, that's $100 to fill up, and it comes out of our hard earned cash that you could be saving. To avoid spending so much cash upfront at the gas pump, people resort to paying for the gas with their credit card. If you put it on a credit card and you are financing your car, your car cost just increased because you are paying a car payment with interest and a credit card payment with interest unless you pay off the credit card monthly.

Purchasing a smaller car that averages 25-30 miles per gallon is a great deal, if it meets your transportation needs. Over time owning a smaller car will save you cash on gas, plus you are being frugal, which allows you to save more money annually. Reflect for a moment on how much you can save per month before making a costly purchase. Buying a car with cash is a paradigm shift in cultural thinking for most Americans. That mindset is different from how many people are traditionally used to thinking and acting. We see and hear car commercials on television that a dealership is giving away cars at 0.0% APR with no money down. When you hear that they want to get you in the dealership and hope you make an impulsive decision to buy. First thing they are going to do is check your credit worthiness and your credit score will determine your interest rate (Annual Percentage Rate (APR)).The credit score is a creation of banks to see who is credit worthy for financing. If banks created and control the credit scoring system and financing, would it be fair to say it is important to learn about banking and money at a deeper level since it impacts our major buying decisions that creates debt for us. Additionally, learning about Wall Street banking, investing, saving, and stocks will help us to better understand the economic influences that impact saving and building wealth.

After the car dealer has you in their dealership, they got you where they want you. Now, it is their mission to keep you in the dealership as long as they can to break you down psychologically to get you to buy the car of your dream. Buying anything of your dream is an illusion that will soon fade. The dealer sells to your emotions as most businesses do. For example, a car sales representative may offer you the color and the new features of your dreams. When you open the car door the scent of the new car smell hits you in the nostril and sends a signal to your brain prompting you to act on your desire. Your senses tell you this is the car for you and the salesman tells you this is the car that fits your dream perfectly.

When you have answered all of their questions on the type of car you were looking for they package that information and offer it back to you to sell you on why you need the car. At this point it is a no brainer, literally, they have you were they want you unless you have the will power to get up and walk out of the dealership. If you decide to stay, it may be because they have hijacked your amygdala or logical decision making capacity, which is your ability to think coherently to make the best decision; all along your gut is sending you alerts that you cannot afford the car or you should not be buying it. In other words, your intuition is speaking to you loudly and clearly, do not do it. If you are not careful, you will continue to tell yourself, I can afford it because I am working with a good company and I am planning to get a nice promotion or pay raise in the near future. You talk yourself into it despite your better judgment, which is inherent in the ego. It happens to the best of us even to the resolute person with a clear focus. Building wealth has to be in the forefront of the mind at all times regardless of how secure we feel in our careers. Being cautious benefits us in the long run.

I am speaking from experience. On many occasions I have talked myself into major purchases that I should not have bought. I have witnessed my love ones get lured into impulsive and glassy eye decision making only to regret it two to three years after the dream has faded and the newness is starting to wane. The ultimate kick in the stomach is when they realize they still have two to three more years remaining of payments to make and they cannot wait for the last payment to be mailed to the bank. Add up all of the possible car payments and think about the money you could save to establish wealth in your lifetime without struggling financially to make ends meet. The potential to save by reducing or eliminating car payment obligations could range from $20,000-$100,000 or more. Placing the savings in the bank or mutual fund can become a reality and the financial stability you deserve. If necessary and where applicable, consider using and staying near public modes of transportation or car pool for a period of time until you are comfortable spending money on a reliable car while preserving your stockpile of cash.

Be cautious of becoming a debtor of banks and car dealers. Too often the dealer takes advantage of the buyer with the cost of the car, taxes, and the finance charges. Your money is what they want and they assume you do not have it on your person when you walk in the door but they do see you as moneybags because they know if your credit is decent, they have a good chance of getting you financed and into a new car. If you finance, you could eventually lose money in interest payments over time if you do not pay off the car loan early; paying it off early is to your advantage.

The finance charges are what you should be aware of if you cannot pay for the car in full. Just know you will be making payments to a bank not the dealership or salesman. The more money you spend on the car the more money you will pay in finance charges.

When you sign the agreement for a new car and then drive the car off the dealers lot, the value of the car declines substantially, which means you just handed over a portion of your potential wealth creation. In many cases, the wealth you handed over to the dealer could be in the range of several thousand dollars. The biggest disappointment is you cannot take the car back to the dealer and get your wealth back. Research shows that you can expect to lose 30-40% of the car value in the first two to three years of ownership. Count that as a loss "L." Instead of giving your wealth away, save it and strongly consider buying a used car in good condition or save to pay cash for a new car.

When you save money from every paycheck you learn the value of hard earn money. Then you will know not to spend it loosely. This lesson is too often learned from the school of hard knocks. When you learn at a young age about money, it is like riding a bike when you become an adult. Good habits stick with you and I am afraid the opposite applies as well, which is the reason so many Americans are strapped for cash and have too little saved.

For example, if you buy a new car for $25,000, you could be upside down as soon as you drive the car off the lot. If you check the car value report at the same dealership, it may be only be worth $19,000 if you try to give the keys back. The average cost of a new car in 2010 is $26,850. The average cost of a used car in 2010 was $8,786. That is a cost difference of $18,064, which is a huge savings that you can keep in your personal savings to help you on your road to accumulating wealth. With a used car, the previous owner absorbs the biggest portion of depreciation.

Another factor to consider when buying a new car over a used car is the taxes you will pay on the new car. There is the state sales tax you pay for new cars that you may not have to pay for when you buy a used car in some states. If you do have to pay for sales tax on a used car it will be substantially less than a new car which could run into the thousands for the new car. Every state sales tax laws are different. In certain situations if you buy from a private seller, you may not have to pay any sales taxes. Additionally, in most states you will have a registration fee. It depends on the year of the car that will determine how much you will pay in states or county fees. Over several years the amount of the annual registration will decrease. If you purchase a used car that is three years old or older, the registration fee and insurance will be substantially less than it would be for a new car.

When buying a used car you do not have to worry about additional dealership options that they add on to the price of the car. In many cases, the additional options and/or features are unnecessary. They do not add value to the car, only extra cost. As an example, do you really need chrome wheels, a wing on the trunk, protective film or heated seats in the third row? When you buy a used car you can search for the car that meets your needs and offers you the features you were looking for not what the dealer thought would "*WOW*" you. Furthermore, if you buy a new car from a dealer you could be charged for shipping, destination fees, and dealer preparation.

When you buy a used car the interest rates are typically higher than a new car. For example, you may have to pay 2-5% interest for a new car over five years and for the used car you may pay 7-10% over five years. Either way it is extra money that you may end up paying if you decide to finance.

To stay ahead of the need to purchase a car it starts with saving money over a period of time. After you have enough money saved, then buy a vehicle that is in good condition at a price that you can honestly afford. If you are unable to pay the full amount in cash, paying a large down payment substantially minimize how much interest you will pay. The more money you pay on the car and the shorter the term of the payment will benefit you in the long run.

To find an affordable car search online and in newspapers for a used vehicle that will meet your needs. There is usually someone within a 100 miles radius that has the car you want with low mileage and in good condition. Nowadays cars can be driven for hundreds of thousands miles without any major problems.

Before you purchase a used car, have it inspected or if it is a pre-certified you should be good to go. Most cars that are within five years old will have a manufacturer's warranty and some dealerships offer a mileage warranty. I encourage you to consider purchasing a warranty at a fair price for at least a few years to be cautious. I would not purchase a warranty after the several years of owning the car if you are okay with making minor repairs to keep the car running. Most car maintenance is oil, brakes, belts, and tires. If you keep up with the maintenance, it will run like new.

A new way of thinking about major purchases is paramount to wealth creation. A new mindset has to be created in the way we view money because it will help us unveil the illusion that a new car will make us happy. Our car is not part of our permanent identity; instead it is a temporary material item that will fade like the paint and wear out like the tires.

Owning a new car does not make us better than anyone. If people like us because of the car we drive, then they are shallow and we might want to distance ourselves from them because they are superficial friends. Friends should accept us based on other characteristics, not the car we drive. Cars are meant to transport us not help us win a popularity contest.

Some people buy expenses cars and still live at home with their parents, which tell me their priorities are out of order. I have heard people with expensive cars tell me they bought an expensive car because they work long hours and they wanted to treat themselves. I understand some people love their jobs and they do not mind working. However, to work overtime hours to pay for an expensive vehicle is a little over the top. The illusion that the latest automobile on the highway will make us happy is an American dream that is debatable. Others are conditioned to want a new car which can be created by our stimulated senses that arouse desire. Couples have separated because one spouse wanted a used car and another spouse wanted a new car. If someone has a strong proclivity for a new car but cannot get it, they act like a child being denied candy or as if they are being tortured. It is amazing how couples, who say they love each other at the altar, and then, begrudgingly go back and forth with each other to come to a compromise on what they should eventually get. Rarely does the decision come down to what is in the best interest of their plan for wealth creation. After a decision is made, one of the spouses feels like they gave in and did not get what they wanted so now you have tension in the relationship. The tension resurfaces in the relationship when another major financial decision arises. Their actions become a tug of war that could have been avoided if both spouses were interested in saving as much money as possible to build wealth. A financial planner would be beneficial to couples by helping them make the best long-term financial decision.

The idea situation would be for automobiles to be more affordable for the majority of Americans (low and middle income earners). 99% of the United States citizens are non-wealthy. As a matter of wealth creation, the wealthy rarely buy new cars; it is all others that are buying new cars every few years.

The wealthy buy cars that they drive for years and their cars maintain value and durability. Some of them lease cars every few years but they can afford to do so, if you are not in the 1% you are wasting your money, energy and labor satisfying your ego. For clarification the 1% is those that earn $250,000 or more annually.

When you do the calculations and pull back the curtain the money you could spend on a car you will see that your money could be better set aside to accumulate wealth. Therefore, strongly consider saving your money for a good used car with low miles. Ideally, we want to save money to create wealth for our family instead of paying it all out on inflated dreams that extreme consumption will make us happy. Buying into the dream delays wealth creation, especially when we buy things we do not necessarily need by financing and/or borrowing. People should not buy a new car unless they have two times the full amount of the car saved. For example, if a car cost $10,000, then you should have at least $20,000 saved so you do not go back to $0. All things should be considered concerning the financial pressures placed on consumers such as increases in gas prices, utilities, and food and job insecurity.

For example, if we were to buy a car at $25,000 at 7% for 60 months, you would pay $4,514 in interest, 6% would be $3,800; and 3% 1,875. Money saved is money earned; the cost savings of buying used versus new could pay for gas over a five year period.

If you decide to purchase a new or used car, put as much down as you possibly can and make extra payments or pay more than the monthly requirement to pay the loan off as soon as possible. Making one extra payment a year towards the principal balance reduces the terms of the loan substantially. Once the car loan is paid off continue to make a car payment to yourself by putting the money into a savings account specifically for your next car purchase so you can pay for it in cash and get the best bottom-line price. Having cash tends to favor the buyer and significantly influences the price when negotiating with the seller.

Benefits of acquiring a used car:

- Lower purchase price
- Lower depreciation
- No or minimal sales tax
- Lower financing costs (fees and interest paid)
- Lower registration and license fee
- Lower insurance premiums

CHAPTER SIX

Reduce Spending and Start Saving

Those who struggle financially struggle because of the lack of knowledge about saving money, investing, banking and money management; young adults through senior citizens fall into that population. KP

An ad from a popular credit card company sent by email during a holiday season stated: "The Holiday Season is a great time to buy a new car. Choose the car or truck of your *dreams*. Get guaranteed low, upfront price-in writing. Pick up your vehicle-without any haggling—from a nearby dealer that's been selected to be a part of our nationwide network. And if you wish, use your card to help pay for part of your purchase. Shop now and drive into the new year with a new car."

The credit card company that was responsible for the advertisement failed to mention the new debt accumulated to repay the money the buyer put on the card and the future payment they would have to make for purchasing the new car. There are hundreds if not thousands of advertisements flooding email inboxes, television and radio and printed on mailings across the nation to buy the car of your *dreams* with no money down. Companies want you to keep dreaming and never wake up to the reality that debt can be bad. Greed and irrationality are equally detrimental to building wealth. When we listen to a commercial we can easily think the economy is stable and jobs are secure. It adds to the illusion of the dream. If consumers were aware of the billions of dollars of debt that is generated by overspending every day, it will sober up many people quickly to the necessity to save more of their money instead of spending it carelessly. I cannot reiterate it enough, the foundation of learning about money and how to save it goes back to how children are raised and taught about money. As a society if we valued financial literacy, the sky would be the limit on what we could achieve. The conversation about teaching children about money should become part of the household, political, and community discussion. If it becomes part of the household discussions, more people may come to realize the positive impact it could have on their lives and others. And, then people may decide to maintain a balance between their work and personal lifestyle by working fewer hours and spending quality time with their children because they have money saved, they own their car and they do not have excessive monthly bills.

Based on data from the Federal Reserve Statistical Release, consumer credit, revolving credit (no specific payoff date, and non-revolving credit (specific payoff dates) continue to increase at alarming rates. There is roughly 10 trillion dollars in revolving and non-revolving credit and the major holders of that outstanding credit are commercial banks, finance companies, credit unions, and pools of securitized assets 7 and 8, i.e. private investors. Private investors are second to commercial banks. Private investors buy debt from banks and profit from the interest paid on the debt. Savvy investors that understand how money works are getting rich at the expense of those in debt. The housing crisis is a testament to the struggle average Americans face. Major Banks and clever investors benefited from the government bailouts and the upside down loans home owners find themselves in. The same applies to credit card debt; investment banks and private investors buy credit card debt and collect money from card holder's interest payments. It's a lot to learn about the inside and outs of the behind the scene investment strategies and money transactions that are made between banks, major investors and credit card companies.

The rich get richer because money makes money. All others have to be wise enough to save and properly manage their money. There is hope for all people to save money and get a head in life. Check the figures on the average amount of money Americans have in a savings account. The figures are low because of overspending, failing to set money to the side to save, and using credit cards. Create a habit of setting money to the side from every check or dollar earned.

If you ever get use to using credit cards to make routine purchases, it can become habitual. To stop using credit cards sometimes it takes a bad financial experience to learn the value of money. Events will happen in life that will bring us closer to our divinity but debt does not have to be one. Deliberate willpower and discipline are needed to form better financial habits. Consumers can become addicts to credit card usage without realizing they are abusing it and themselves. A credit card rehabilitation program or counseling might be necessary to stop the psychological dependency on credit cards to curb spending. If a therapist is needed, seek assistance without feeling embarrassed.

Many Americans are couch potatoes, which makes them an easy target to be influenced by advertisements and the media. Americans are known to spend hours in front of the television. Too many consumers allow the media to create their course of action. To create personal wealth we have to be vigilant of the plethora of messages that have a purpose to influence our behavior to consume; there is peer pressure and there is media pressure. To build wealth, a higher purpose to save has to supersede our feeling to spend by keeping us on a path to perpetually save money. The importance and purpose for saving have to be ingrained in our mentality.

Credit cards were essentially nonexistent when I was growing up in the 80's and early 90's. They were not part of the shopping experience or monthly expenses. My parents did not have a credit card and they lived comfortably within their means. If they did not have the money, they would let you know they did not have the money, which meant you did not get the item until they could pay for it with cash.

Initially, credit cards were created for the travel and entertainment industry in 1958. At that time card holders had to pay the full balance each month. Over a period of time, banks expanded usage to include revolving credit which allowed credit card holders to pay a portion of the balance each month. In the late 1980s, American Express, Discover, Visa and Mastercard lead the credit revolution. People living in the United States were in the midst of a silent revolution while the change was in progress in the banking and business world that would eventually affect household's budgets and saving power. The introduction of credit cards to the masses broke down consumers' reservations to overspend and disciplines to save.

In the early 1990s, credit cards start flooding mailboxes unsolicited with different tactics to entice consumers to sign up. Some banks and credit card companies offered attractive offers to get people to signup, i.e. low interest or no interest and modest credit limits. They offered points for purchases that would allow card holders to receive cash back or use the points to buy gifts from an in-house catalog. From the onset they intended to stimulate consumer spending, which is a mirror reflection of m-commerce; the next consumerism revolution.

If young people and adults are committed to financial literacy, saving money, and establishing financial stability, they would have to get engaged with learning as much as they can about what is evolving in commerce, which would guard them against being taking advantage of. Consumers would be cognizant of the marketing antics and fees associated with credit card ownership and utilization.

A citizenry educated about finances would understand the interest schedule for late payments or offer termination dates. They would also know how to protect themselves from attractive credit card and loan offers. The opposite happens when the populace is not astute about the vices of credit card companies and bank practices. Too often adults are indifferent to banking practices. The speed at which things are changing in the economy, individuals should avoid becoming a victim of alluring credit card and loan invitations as well as excessive spending.

Many people from eastern countries deflect the forces of resorting to using banks and signing up for credit cards because of their cultural values to save money and live within their income. If they do borrow money, they borrow it from family members or tribal members, which can come with severe obligations to repay as well as maintaining respect in their social circle or community. Western banks and credit card companies have tried to penetrate eastern countries foreign banking systems but they have faced many challenges. For example, you will hardly see foreigners from China, India, Ghana, Korea, and Turkey, in your local bank or shopping with a credit card. Wherever western civilization banking practices have influenced banking practices in other countries, banking and monetary problems have surfaced, i.e. Greece, France, Europe, Portugal, Italy, Spain, Lithuania, and Ireland just to name a few. While China has become a super power by saving money and then loaning it to the United States.

Limit using plastic to shop

With increased utilization of debit cards and credit cards, fees are bound to increase. As banks look for ways to increase revenue, fees will spike. The Durbin Alexander Amendment changed the game on credit card fees that banks can charge. That left debit cards users vulnerable to seeing an increase in debit cards fees. Reverting to spending cash helps reduce spending and fees paid to the bank. Based on information from a banking report, the average minimum balance required to avoid a monthly fee rose from $249 in 2010 to $585 in 2011, an increase of nearly 135 percent. ATM fees are have increased 3 percent, if you do not use an in-network or your banks ATM machines you could pay $5 or more in fees after you pay your bank's fee and the ATM sponsored bank fee.

It is hard for the average person to resist credit card companies, because credit card companies are dialed into how to market to our emotional state with marketing strategies and pitches that capture our attention. If you start receiving many credit card offers in the mail repeatedly; just know you are being targeted for excessive consumption. They know who is likely to sign up and shop. Naturally, if we receive a request or invitation enough time, our natural defenses get weaker and give in to the offer. It is similar to a child constantly asking for something until they get it. Credit card companies know the average number of times they need to send a mailing to you before you accept their offer. Their hope is at some point you will need a credit line to cover expenses. It could be that you are in need of a vacation. Seeing enough offers can create an illusion that we cannot live without a credit card. Fortunately, personal check cards with a credit card logo have reduced the need for credit cards, especially if you have saved cashed. Banks can create illusions that are powerful which are part of the overall marketing strategies to get the targeted individual to sign on the dotted line. They can be relentless but you have the right to tell them to back off.

When people start using credit cards, they think they will pay the balance off monthly or as soon as they receive extra money, i.e. tax refund or bonus. However, before they realize it, the balance on the card increases or an emergency occurs that exhaust their funds, which was money earmarked to pay off the credit card balance. In this common scenario, the credit card balance still exists and they are left making monthly payments.

Murphy's Law: if something can happen, it will happen, just when you least expect it.

Murphy's Law does not happen all the time but when it does, it is unwelcomed. Then once again you find yourself having to pay monthly payment with interest until you can pay back the debt.

Creditcard.com is a good source to find out average credit card interest rates. In 2011 the average was 15%. If you decided to pay the minimum payment, it could take three times as long to pay the balance. Banks and credit card companies profit significantly from credit card users when they only pay the minimum payment and late fees. Late fees and interest charges are significant revenue streams for banks and credit card companies. Based on a study conducted by the Office of Comptroller of the Currency found that in January 2010 $901 million was collected in late fees compared to $427 million in November 2010, which was a significant drop after new federal regulations on how much banks and credit card companies could charge customers for late fees. Lenders collected an astounding $7 billion in 1996 and $10 billion in 2003. Thanks to legislation approved by law makers the amount of interest and late fees banks and credit card companies can charge have steadily declined; government intervention is often the mechanism to slow down the abuse by banks and credit card companies.

My recommendation is an unconventional approach, which is to avoid credit cards as best as possible because of the potential to use it for non-emergencies. If you never get one, you never know what you are missing. If you do get one, it could create feelings of guilt and regret after the fact and years later. If millions of young adults would make that commitment, the debt trends in the United States would decline drastically.

I will admit my ignorance about saving and gullibility about credit cards caused me to go overboard on spending. It happens. Money lenders paint a rosy picture of experiencing the life of your best dreams. They fail to share with you that the dream can easily become a nightmare if you fail to pay timely, miss a payment or only pay the minimal payment.

Where are the testimonies of people that are trying to rebuild their credit and livelihood after filing Chapter 11 personal bankruptcy or the millions of stories each year of individuals that become indebted to credit card companies, money lenders, and banks? Those stories are ignored and sweep under the rug. In 2011 more than 1 million people filed for bankruptcy. I think money lenders should be required to balance the advertisement like pharmaceuticals are required to tell the benefits and side effects when they advertise; maybe that will get consumer's attention before signing a credit or loan application and cause them to change their mind. It is almost like meeting *Rumpelstiltskin*. You are now in a challenging situation because you have to repay the money you never had but should have had in the bank to cover expenses and handle emergencies. Instead, you are living paycheck to paycheck and waiting for the next check to arrive to pay on the bill.

Do not be overwhelmed if it happens to you because it is unfortunately common for Americans to be plagued with debt. You do not have to look far for examples just consider the debt of the nation. Fortunately, debt is not life ending, so remain hopeful through the circumstance and learn from the experience and live to tell the story. Your credit score maybe negatively impacted but that is a temporary inconvenience. In 2 to 7 years you can recover and in the timeframe save your cash for a stronger financial future. When you awaken to the reality of what debt can do to you consider it a revelation or a new birth and then help others prevent financial calamity.

If you absolutely have to have a credit card, I recommend having enough cash saved that will cover the credit limit. At a minimal you should have that amount saved, having more saved would be better. Paying the balance in full is highly recommended. At all cost, restrict using a credit card because the goal is to save money. If you are dumping all of your money to pay a balance every month, it will be difficult to save and pay other living expenses. Hopefully, you see the importance or the wisdom in living within your means. You can save more money by keeping more of it and by spending less of it.

Magazines and newspapers occasionally share stories of people that have overspent, in debt and trying to get their finances back on track. There was an article I read about a lady who was a divorced mother of three children who could scarcely make ends meet despite making a decent salary and receiving a decent pay raise from her employer. She had several credit cards with a total credit card debt of nearly $12,000. She was only able to make the monthly minimum payments; she was working overtime, unable to invest in her company 401k, and unable to enjoy life. After receiving advice from a financial planner, she was able to start reducing her credit card debt one card at a time, which is called the "snowball effect." Her financial planner shared with her to pay extra on one credit card at a time to eliminate the smallest balance first, and then apply the same approach to the next card. She found herself struggling more when she had a sudden decline in monthly income.

Reductions in salary or supplemental income have been known to weaken a person's financial position; many Americans live paycheck to paycheck with too little saved in an emergency account. Financial advisors warn that if someone has a credit card, they will at least go through this experience once, which is unfortunate. Divorce is equally as bad because it has been labeled as one of the highest expense in a person's life. This story is common in American because of the number of credit cards per household and the high divorce rate; 50% of marriage ends in divorce.

When you have a consumer nation people rarely save money. Consequently, when it is time to buy a house other major purchases such as furniture or an automobile people have to borrow money and that leads to paying more for the purchase in the long run and less money to save.

Since 2007, millions of people have lost their jobs. At the end of December 2011, there were over 13 million people unemployed. Many of the unemployed are new college graduates. Others were just starting their career while others are middle age or near retirement. The middle age and near retirement workers have the most at stake because of their age and household expenses. This is the reason I advocate securing your financial future with liquid cash as a foundation so you can be prepared in the event of a company restructuring that may send you packing to look for another job elsewhere. In today's economy with rapid and constant change, no job is secure.

A portion of the millions of people out of work are entrepreneurs that had construction companies. They have been mainly affected by the down turn in construction projects. Another group of people affected by the down economy had a primary residence and a second home. If both spouses were not downsized possibly one of the spouses was and that seriously impacted their household income and their ability to meet their financial responsibilities. Many couples were living off of two incomes. They overstretched themselves by wanting more than what was necessary to live comfortably. My household income afforded me the opportunity to live on one income comfortably until I decided to take a shot at purchasing investment properties with the expectations that the housing market would continue to rise in value. My greatest fear became real when I was laid off after 10 years of dedicated service and stellar performance. When companies want to trim their payroll and other expenses they will find a way to restructure the organization, which is a nightmare for those that are laid-off; especially, if they have overextended themselves financially and have less than nine months of cash reserved for such events. If they have saved wisely, then it is easier for them to pay expenses until they can secure another opportunity. They do not have to settle for a less than a desirable opportunity.

Reduce Spending and Start Saving

For 24-Hour Customer Service Call 1-800-███████

████████████ CARD
VISA

Prepared For	KEVIN D POWELL
Account Number	███████████
Statement Closing Date	02/27/12
Credit Line	$2,500
Available Credit	$0

Send Inquiries To:

Send Payments To:
PAYMENT REMITTANCE CENTER ████████

Account Summary

Previous Balance	$2,138.77
- Credits	$0.00
- Payments	$298.00
+ Purchases & Other Charges	$50.00
+ Cash Advances	$0.00
+ FINANCE CHARGE	$45.12
= New Balance	$1,935.89

Payment Information

New Balance	$1,935.89
Current Payment Due	$114.00
Past Due Amount	$47.00
Total Amount Due	$161.00
Current Payment Due Date	03/23/12

Your Past Due Amount of $47.00 is due immediately.
Your Current Payment of $114.09 is due 03/23/12

For your records:

Amount Paid	
Check Number	
Date Paid	

Rate Information

IF YOU WISH TO PAYOFF YOUR BALANCE IN FULL,
THE BALANCE NOTED ON YOUR STATEMENT IS NOT THE PAY OFF AMOUNT. PLEASE CALL ██████████ FOR PAYOFF INFORMATION
YOUR RATE MAY VARY ACCORDING TO THE TERMS OF YOUR AGREEMENT

Type of Balance	ANNUAL INTEREST RATE	DAILY FINANCE CHARGE RATE	AVERAGE DAILY BALANCE	PERIODIC FINANCE CHARGES	TRANSACTION FINANCE CHARGES	TOTAL FINANCE CHARGES
PURCHASES	25.990%	.07120%	$2,044.44	$45.12	$0.00	$45.12
CASH ADVANCES	25.990%	.07120%	$0.00	$0.00	$0.00	$0.00
TOTAL				$45.12	$0.00	$45.12

Days In Billing Cycle 31

Important Information

YOUR ACCOUNT IS PAST DUE. IF THE PAYMENT HAS NOT ALREADY BEEN SENT,
PLEASE REMIT THE TOTAL AMOUNT DUE TODAY OR CALL US AT ██████████

TOTAL "FINANCE CHARGE" BILLED IN 2011 $574.91
TOTAL "FINANCE CHARGE" PAID IN 2011 $538.97

This Account is closed to future transactions.

Transactions

Trans	Post	Reference Number	Description	Credits	Charges
02/06	02/06	███████████	BRANCH PAYMENT CHECK REF# DZEM6JYFMV	125.00	
02/23	02/23	███████████	BRANCH PAYMENT CHECK REF# DZEMRVQMUD	173.00	
02/27	02/27		LATE CHARGE		50.00
		PERIODIC "FINANCE CHARGE"	PURCHASES $45.12 CASH ADVANCE $0.00		45.12

See reverse side for important information.

5596 8087 VTG   1   7 19 126227 8   F D PAGE 1 of 1   14 5921 1660 BNDC 01005596   5685

Tips for getting out of debt:

- Make paying off debt a top priority

- Establish a budget -- and start to save

- Use rewards to stay motivated

- Allocate 1 percent of your pre-tax earnings -- or

  about $25 a month -- toward your 401(k)

- Focus on knocking down your smallest debt first.

  Paying off just one debt is a great relief

- When you invest in yourself, there's less money to

  allocate to spending.

CHAPTER SEVEN

Purchasing a Home

"Americans now know that housing prices can go down and they can go down by 10, 20, 30, and in some cases, 40 or 50 percent. We know they can go down. But five years ago, we thought they could only go up." Bill Gross

I remember when my wife and I bought our first house. I can honestly say without embarrassment that I had saved less than the minimum amount required to put down on the house. I had to take money out of my retirement account to go towards the down payment, which was less than 20 percent of the sell price. In most cases first time home buyers are allowed to put less than 20 percent down, which means you will have to pay primary mortgage insurance (PMI) for several years until the equity value of the home is worth 20 percent. PMI usually is an extra fee added to the monthly payment that could cost 2% of the price of the house for several years.

Fortunately, I qualified for the first time home buyers program which meant I could pay 5% down plus pay closing costs. I put down approximately $8,000 and closing was approximately $4,000. I had not saved properly prior to buying a home. The small amount of liquid money I had saved, I ended up spending it all on the house and pending wedding. Consequently, I exhausted my savings account. Before buying the home I was spending frivolously on entertainment and dining. Looking back on the situation I should have saved more money before buying the house so I would have had money left in my savings account for emergencies and to have liquid cash on hand. Without thinking, I put myself in a position to live paycheck to paycheck and resort to credit cards. At the time, I had an American Express to which I paid off monthly. However, I made enough money that I did not have to put myself in that situation. All I had to do was buy a smaller home for less money or saved a lot more money to pay greater than 20% down for the house.

When I acquired the home in 2003, it was during a seller's market, which meant I spent more money on the house than I should have. The housing market was so hot the year I bought my house I found myself in bidding wars with other buyers. After making two offers on others homes, I was determined to win the bid on the house I eventually purchased.

As I was preparing to sign the documents for the home my gut feeling was I should have saved more money to pay towards the down payment, plus enough to cover home improvements or upgrades. I was starting to regret not saving more. Later I realized I was not a smart home buyer because I should have been able to pay extra money per month towards the principal balance to pay the mortgage off sooner than 30 years. By paying extra monthly payments towards the principal, the payoff timeframe could have been reduced to 10-15 years.

At some point in my life as a young adult, I should have been trained to think about saving for buying a home and paying it off within 15 years. Instead, like many we are left to figure things out by trial and error, at the last minute when a decision needs to be made or after the fact, which is the consequence of improper financial training and guidance.

Now I realize that I was not taught to think about planning for major financial and life events that are common in a person's life. Like many, I was ignorant and illiterate about saving and making financial decisions, which is why I strongly believe financial education should be taught to children at an early age. There are things we will eventually want and need to do in life such as attend college, obtain a home and furniture, get married, have children, and buy a car. Nothing is new under the sun but the average young person is not thinking long-term about these things and each generation fails to train the next generation; therefore the cycle is perpetual for many generations. Many people will reach a certain point in life and reflect on their prior decisions with clarity about what they should have done differently or earlier in life to prepare for events that occur later in life. I have found the key to long-term financial success is to live modestly, save money persistently, start saving early in life and be patient.

During the years of 2000-2007 the housing market was booming. Homes only stayed on the market for a few days before they were sold to eager buyers. These buyers were investors or people looking for a primary residence. It was also during this time when banks or mortgage companies were offering consumers mortgage programs that required minimal down payments to purchase a house. These mortgage programs were a trap for many people that could not afford the home. They had a mortgage with a balloon effect. After a few years the interest rate would increase every few years. After the first mortgage increase many people could no longer afford their home. Home buyers doing this time were hoping to buy and sell in a few years to make a profit. Unfortunately, the housing bubble bust and many people were left with unfavorable loans.

It has been reported that banks and mortgage companies targeted a segment of the population with high risk mortgage loans. It's hard to believe people would do that. Like most businesses, they know where to find people that want relief from financial burdens in this case from high risk mortgages. Banks and mortgage companies were eventually accused of predatory lending. Interestingly, I discovered that banks and mortgage companies had been accused and warned of predatory mortgage lending in the late 1990's. They did not stop then, they continued through 2007 and they will try it again because history has a way of repeating itself depending on the administration in the White House and the politicians in congress.

Many foreclosures and personal bankruptcies are a result of a decade of bad mortgages. High risk mortgages did not create themselves instead they were created by greed. Some Banks and debt investors profited from high risk mortgages, which is the reason for the startup of Wall Street sit-ins. Banks were bailed out of the mortgage crisis while tax payers and consumers with bad mortgages had to suffer the consequences of the mortgage crisis, which is sad because anyone over the age of 18 that is not educated about money and finances are susceptible to falling into the hands of predatory lenders. Each time it happens they will be excused of not being financially responsible, the onus is on the individual not the financial institutions that created and underwrote the mortgage.

For a couple of years of owning my home I had an interest only loan until I sold my home in 2009. Initially, I had a 30 year fixed conventional loan. The reason I signed up for the interest only mortgage loan, like many others it was peer pressure; plus, I was planning to sell my home in a year or two to buy another house to meet the needs of my growing family. When I refinanced to get the interest only loan, I received a home equity line of credit as well. This was the third life event that set me up for debt. The first was father a child before getting married; the second was buying a home in a seller's market without putting more than 20% down at closing.

Many banks were offering attractive home equity loans at low interest rates and low refinancing fees. It was a common business practice prior to 2008. Now interest only mortgage loans are a fragment in American history because many homes are valued less than what is owed on the property.

Home owners have seen the equity in their home substantially decrease. Analyst have reported, "that consumers have lost the flexibility of being able to finance their debt through home equity lines of credit and are now moving those balances over to credit cards. And those typically have a higher minimum payment amount, and consequently, consumers are running into a credit squeeze and running up delinquencies." Consequently, many people are walking away from their dream homes and homes they thought they would eventually sell for a huge profit, only to be left with dashed dreams and a pile of debt.

Prior to the 2008 housing bust, I enjoyed watching home improvement television shows on how to buy low and sale high (flip homes). Television stations glamourized and popularized buying and selling homes. Because it was television, you rarely saw the ugly side of bad deals, angry new home owners that discovered problems with the loan or homes that were unable to be repaired or improved to their liking after the house flipper bought the house. Not to mention they did not show all of the paperwork and fees associated with buying and selling a house. That's Hollywood for you. It is never good to air dirty laundry on television if you want the show to have good ratings for commercial advertisements, which is where the big bucks gets poured into the coffers of the television companies that generate sales from companies advertising.

I admit I was a fan of those shows and I participated in buying and selling investment properties. After seeing it done over and over again on television with ease, I got a home equity line of credit. At that point my ability to control my spending was undone. I was anxiously looking forward to upgrading my kitchen and bathrooms. Writing checks from the home equity line of credit made me feel rich because I could spend thousands of dollars to add perceived value to my home. I eventually upgraded my kitchen with granite countertops and stainless steel appliances. The appliances and the countertop I replaced were in good condition, which is the absurdity. However, I felt like I was doing the right thing because I was adding perceived value to the home. Plus, I figured I would get the money back whenever I decided to sell it.

As time went on and I still had money available from the home equity line of credit, I bought two properties that I am still paying mortgages on that I have been unable to sell. As you can imagine, my savings has been severely devastated. Before selling my home, I witnessed the value drop despite adding the upgrades and my investment properties dropped in value significantly.

With millions of people in the United States affected by the housing bust, few people expected the housing bubble to burst when it did and I was one of them. There was little notice, if any, from media outlets that it was going to happen. It caught many hard working and honest Americans off guard. When the bell tolled on the housing market, it came crashing down. It was abrupt and merciless to the American home owner, small construction companies, real estate businesses and anyone else that had an association with homes. Americans were fanatical with buying and selling homes up until the point of the stock market crash of 2008.

During the housing boom it was easy for real estate agents to sell homes because buyers were ready to buy without any much effort on the part of the real estate agent. Deals fell into their laps. No selling strategies or tactics were needed to bring in buyers. Now, real estate agents are being challenged to bring in buyers and sell homes. Many real estate agents are only as good as a bull market. I have had to learn that the hard way.

Prior to 2008 the real estate market was flooded with real estate agents. Many people were jumping on the bandwagon to make a quick buck. That has changed as of late and agents are leaving the industry in droves because it is not the lucrative career field it once was when buyers would walk into a real estate agents office and sign the paperwork to purchase a house in the same day. Some real agents received multiple bids for the same house and I am sure some real estate agents pretended to have another offer only to get the buyer that made an offer to sweeten the pot on the table.

Many mortgage companies went out of business and people lost their jobs when the housing market declined. I knew people who were purchasing $600,000 homes and they were only making $120,000 per year in total household income. In addition to their large mortgage payment they had property and city taxes to pay as well as association's fees and homeowner insurance. If the working spouse or the *"bread winner"* were to lose his or her job, they would have been in a tough financial situation. Then they would hope one of them would be able to find another job making equal or more money to meet their financial obligations.

When you have a high unemployment like the one the United States has been experiencing since 2008, 9% nationally and as high as 11% in certain states, high paying jobs are scarce and harder to obtain. This is something that young people should keep in mind when thinking about purchasing a home or buying luxury items. The economy or loss of employment could occur at any time. It is like building your future on uncertainty in the market because you are taking a risk on your job being around for 30 years which is the average life of a mortgage. Or that the economy will be stable enough at least in the industry you are working in over the life span of your mortgage. After this economic ordeal, we cannot shrug off these realities or turn a blind eye to *"what if"* you lose your job. This is why it is vitally important for financial literacy to be taught to younger generations and our children at a young age so they can prepare themselves financially for any instability in their career or the economy. Everyone that works should take it seriously to set aside at least six to nine months income to live comfortable in case of an emergency or loss of job.

Dr. Martin Luther King, Jr. stated we should try to live within our means. He also stated if a person is interested in purchasing a home, it should be no more than two times his/her salary or household income. Dr. King was passionate about economic empowerment and he was light years ahead of his time. His advice was profound and more important to follow. If I had heard Dr. King's message prior to purchasing my home, I would have offered a lower price or found a home in my price range instead of growing into the mortgage payment. If I had heeded his advice I wonder what neighborhood I would have lived in in New Jersey where the home prices and taxes are some of the highest in the country. Young people have to make decisions that are grounded in logic and sound advice because every situation and housing market can be slightly different.

Since Dr. King's advice, housing prices have skyrocketed. However, since the housing bust, you can find a modest home at a very low price; many homes are well under the market price and desperate home owners are ready to sell to get from under the mortgage burden. There are ebbs and flows in housing prices. Therefore, buy conservatively to be able to save money to build wealth.

The questions many Americans are asking themselves during this economic recession is do they really need a *mini-mansion*, 3,000 square foot home with five bedrooms, a three car garage, four bathrooms, and extra-large walk-in closets. People are rethinking their priorities and values. They want a simpler lifestyle, realizing that they may have gone overboard by buying mini-mansions. When they purchased the home, they were hoping it would receive a sizable profit when they sold it or that it would secure their retirement.

When you get caught in the energy of the nation by doing what everyone else is doing, it is hard to remain focus on what you are able to afford. Then after the transaction, you ask yourself the question, "what have I done." Ignorance is bliss and seems like wisdom about these things is scarce because many Americans (99%) seem to be in the same boat rowing in the same direction by following the shallow trends of the moment, instead of thinking independently about their individual situation.

An indication of the national trend is the government continues to raise the national debt ceiling and consumers continue to increase their personal debt burden. Experience has taught me that ignorance can lead to performing actions that degrade your personality, which can cause sleepless night and persistent headaches also known as pain and misery. Where there is perceived pleasure, pain is close by. Therefore, stay neutral and objective as much as possible in life while seeking to correct your faults and purify your heart. Do not get emotionally attached to anything because everything is impermanent. Physical things like animated beings fade away over time. Only the soul of the person remains. It is important for it to be nourished and contented. Fortunately, our soul does not require much in the form of material things and adventure.

When you decide to purchase your first home consider purchasing a home that can be paid off in 10-15 years. Once it is paid off you can decide if you want to keep it or sell it. Be sure to put down greater than 20% on the first purchase. If you decide to sell, take the money from the sell and apply all of it to the new home. Then strive to pay off the new home in 10 to15 years. After the home is paid for, you can pay yourself by placing the money in a savings account indefinitely. The purchase of a home can be one of the biggest expenses a person will make in their lifetime. Paying a 30 year mortgage only benefits the bank when you consider how much money you will pay over the life of the loan in interest. Think about how much money you could put into your bank account and save if you pay your mortgage off early. Remember the goal is to save more money so you can establish financial security and build wealth for future generations.

CHAPTER EIGHT

Rethink Spending

You can have too much money that you do not know what to do with it. That can be a good thing with proper knowledge and discipline. There is more charity that can be done with money than without it. KP

Consumers are being driven towards using mobile credit cards and instant checkout in place of using cash. Be on guard with spending as mobile commerce and mobile wallet becomes main stream and more popularized with the arrival of high tech smart phones, tablets, and iPads. Banks and your favorite retailers want and will have access to your personal information. The applications we are able to download and link to via mobile applications are looking after their financial interest not ours. If you are ever in a situation where you cannot pay your bills, your bank or the credit card company might have access and a legal right to debt your account to pay the bill automatically.

When we download retailers' application on our smart phones and tablet pc, they have knowledge of where we are at all times. The age old cliché, "You can run but you cannot hide" rings true today with mobile commerce. Big Brother retailer has the software capabilities to be tracking us at all times and tracking our historical spending patterns between shopping experiences; even while we are sleep they are there. When we wake-up we will be alerted to the deals of the day. A 24/7 surveillance is not the big brother we dreamed of having watch over us, our money nor our spending patterns. With financial literacy we should be able to watch over ourselves. Credit, debits, trading, and cash make the world go around in an economical system, which is the world we live in, so businesses are tasked with outsmarting consumers so they can increase their profits to pay shareholders, investors and the company CEO millions of dollars.

President of a boutique flash sales site based out of Boston, states, "2011 is certainly the year that mobile broke out and the results have been absolutely incredible." "Last January, mobile was 2 percent of our sales and this holiday season, one out of three sales is coming via mobile," he said. "Every month I think we've hit a high in terms of mobile growth and the next month it keeps growing…mobile is a huge bright spot and a critical factor in driving the growth. It takes the prize as being the largest driver of our growth this year." The same organization saw almost a 200 percent increase in mobile sales on Cyber Monday compared with a year ago. In early December 2011, sales grow more than 250 percent. "With one in three sales transacting via mobile, 40 to 50 percent of that is iPad specifically," the president of the company said, "of the other 50 to 60 percent that is mobile, Apple devices dominate and account for about 90 percent." An online payment transaction company said they saw a 397% increase in the number of consumers using their mobile devices on Cyber Monday 2011 compared to 2010. The momentum for excessive mobile spending is building and coming at you like an express train; it is loaded with a lot of extra subtle pressure for us to spend. Once the fever for mobile payments, shopping, and marketing becomes ingrained in our culture, it will be hard to side step it because it becomes the new way of living.

According to a 2011 survey, 87% of tablet owners shopped during the Christmas holiday using their tablet pc and spent an average of $325 per transaction. Tablets owners cite convenience and ease of use as reasons why they like to shop via the devices. More than half of tablet owners say shopping makes them feel happy and more excited, indulgent and generous than other forms of online, mobile or in-store shopping.

A consumer matrix exists. It is hard to deny and circumvent it without proper financial education and monetary literacy. The financial matrix is driven by complex and simple economics, i.e. profits and losses, profits and earnings, and dollars and cents = net gain. The financial matrix is constantly being tweaked to capture a larger segment of consumers' hard earned dollars. Subsequently, it is easy to get in over your head with debt and numerous routine bills. If you find yourself in a financial challenging situation reach out to a credit counselor, non-profit debt management organization, your bank, credit card supplier(s), or a love one about the situation. Many banks and credit card companies have hardship programs. They can reduce the interest rate, monthly payment amount, or settle the balance for a lesser amount than what is owed. Credit counselors may be able to provide financial advice and assistance with working with the lending institution. They can share money management tips and negotiate terms with the bank or Credit Card Company. Some counselors are free and there are some that charge a fee. Find a counseling agency that meets your needs.

Do not blame yourself for the situation or be hard on yourself for falling in the trap that millions of Americans have fallen into and will continue to fall in. The illusion of joy and happiness that advertisements create is very powerful and convincing. Our vigilance and aptitude to guard against the deception is necessary at all times. Go easy on yourself, take a deep breath, take one day at a time and learn from your financial mistakes. Make a personal commitment that once you get out of the situation you will not let it happen to you again.

I ended up with business credit card debt because of trying to operate a small business. I saw my credit card balance increase or stay virtually the same without being able to pay it down and I have been late paying the bill. I have found myself in uncomfortable financial situations but I have been resolute in my purpose that it would not break me; instead I decided to take it on the chin, learn from my experience, and share it with the world. As a result, I am more resolute to save cash and help others prevent financial misfortune and avoid potential financial pitfalls that exist so they can build wealth and be able to help others. My story is similar to too many hard working Americans.

Young people and aspiring entrepreneurs have to be extra careful. Banks and credit card companies are waiting for you to walk through their doors needing a loan or to fill out a credit card application. Entrepreneurs are within lenders scope because entrepreneurs are viewed as gamblers, risk takers, and optimistic spenders. Few entrepreneurs go into business with the attitude that they are going to fail and lenders know that which makes entrepreneurs an easy target. If you are considering being an entrepreneur, be observant and prepared before you go into a bank to open a checking and savings account to say no to signing a credit card application unless you really know what you are getting into.

The same rule applies to a young person; if you do not have 2 – 3 times the amount of the credit limit in your savings, training in money management and discipline, politely say no thank you to the banker when presented with a credit card application.

Statistics show that most businesses fail within the first few years of operation and those companies increase or exhaust their business credit line in an attempt to keep the business afloat. A key caveat for entrepreneurs to remember is you are on the hook for the credit card balances that are due. Although you signed the credit card application using your company name, you are a personal guarantor that the debt will be paid.

The reality of debt can be sobering. Learning from the school of hard knocks is not fun which is the reason I wrote this book and advocate for early childhood through adulthood financial education. Early financial literacy has the potential to strengthen our nation and world. It has been my lot in life to go through what has been written about and then to reflect on the situations to share my insight and experience. If young people are not taught the right way, how will they know the way to go? God has given me the responsibility and talents to share my experience and help young people from making the same money mistakes I have made and that millions of people make yearly. Lack of financial literacy is a major contributor to financial blunders. Ambition and desire are contributing factors as well.

There are no short cuts in life and when you think there is a short cut triple check and do not make a hasty financial decision without money to pay for it. Pray on it and search inwardly for patience, guidance, wisdom and contentment. Deals that look and sound too good to be true, usually are gimmicks to get your money. Stay focus on saving it.

We have to envision ourselves as being empowered to resist our desires. We have to rebuff being like the masses that over spend. Otherwise, we risk spending our income on too many bills and unnecessary expenses. When we split our paychecks to pay bills we weaken our saving power. It is like having one slice of bread instead of the whole loaf. When we have many financial obligations, i.e. utilities, mortgage, car payment, water, grocery, college tuition, entertainment, credit cards, insurance, gas, etc., income diminishes quickly. Try feeding 10 people with a 12" pizza, it will be a challenge to have any left for yourself unless you feed yourself first or hoard it. Do not spread your monthly income thin; hoard it. Save a high percentage of it.

If you have bills, it is prudent to pay them timely. However, it is not always practical if you are overextended. If you miss too many credit card payments with the bank that holds your personal funds, they have the legal right to deduct money from your personal account to cover the minimum amount owed. It happened to me so I am speaking from experience. I never read the fine print of the credit card application but the late payment details are in there. When it happened I was surprised to say the least. That experienced taught me new lessons about personal banking issued credit cards like do not have a credit card with the bank that you bank with. Many people take for granted the small print because of their eagerness to sign up for a credit card or loan. Incidents like this happen too often to young adults and naïve credit card holders.

There are many websites that provide tips and helpful information on living debt free and how to save money. They will be able to provide assistance and give you advice on who you should contact if they are unable to assist you. Recognizing the need to get professional assistance is a major step in the process to eliminate debt. Debt should be taking seriously. People that should have credit cards are those that can pay the balance monthly and save a decent percentage of their monthly income. That means disposable income and stable employment. Earning a high salary is helpful but it is not a guarantee to build wealth. High salary earners should keep in mind that they are dispensable; consequently, they should have at least eight to twelve months of income saved. A high salary does not make you wealthy. If you lose your high paying job it may take a year or more to find a job that pays equal or more than you were earning. It may take several years to get back to the previous level of income. If your living expenses are exorbitant and you do not have the savings to cover them, you will need to be prepared and plan for recovery confidently and diligently; never give up and remain calm. Time has a way of healing. Remember, you are not alone. In

2011 there were 13 million Americans officially unemployed and 25 million Americans actual unemployed. Some economist would say the unemployment numbers were higher than 25 million. I continue to read about large and small companies laying-off employees because of organizational restructuring. The companies I read about have historically been known to pay their employees well. Money spent and not saved circulates back to the rich and then slowly filters back down.

We have to reexamine our saving and spending habits. Our children naturally learn our habits by observing and mimicking what we do. It becomes natural for them to repeat what they have learned. To train our children properly about finances, we have to strengthen our personal financial position, build our personal savings account and live by example daily by trimming expenses and using cash for purchases.

It can all start today by making a personal commitment that you will live contentedly, peacefully, and make every effort to save more cash. Finally, look for ways to build a financial support group and inspire others to join the group to help each other save more cash and avoid and/or eliminate debt. You can do it. I believe in you; more importantly, believe in yourself!

Visit: **www.kdpowell.wordpress.com** and **www.moneymanagement.org** for tips on saving money and eliminating debt

http://www.usdebtclock.org

EPILOGUE

Learn to save a high percentage of your income. Do not get caught up in the seduction of consumerism and materialism. Be creative with saving money. Car pool or share a house (apartment) with others if necessary to save more money. Create a second or third income if necessary. Spending and saving are conscious decisions. Think of a certain percentage that you want to go in a special savings for yourself. That could be 50% of your check. There is no limit on how much you can save unless you impose the limit on yourself by over spending. Make yourself rich instead of companies. They have enough money and they are rich enough. Set up your lifestyle for you to save as much as you can. If you go to work to earn a living, pay your body for having to put forth the effort to get up and work the hours required to make a living. What is the value you put on your body and brain power?

In our society, we are taught to get a job, and then acquire items we want before we have the money to pay for them, instead of having the cash up front and then make the purchase. There are people that do not own anything you see them with; instead it is owned by the banks because it is being financed. This is how the cycle of debt and poverty are perpetuated year after year and generation after generation. Many people die without a burial policy and family members have to scramble up the money to pay for the burial. It happens too often in our communities and families. It is evident when businesses announce to the public through advertisements zero percent interest payments for 12 months with no money down and credit is same as cash but it is cash we do not have, it is cash that we are working towards earning in the future. It is the carrot and stick principle. As long as you can see the carrot, business will make you work hard to obtain it. Therefore, we have to be thinking about working to save money for ourselves and postpone the other stuff until it is deeply discounted and we have the cash to pay for it.

Debt can be a burden on the mind and weigh heavy on the soul. Debt can drive people to death. It can be like the one ton elephant on your back. I have also found it can be like hornets that constantly sting and swarm around your head until it or you are eliminated. Prevent the latter by nipping debt in the bud early by not incurring it through overspending. The world outside of you does not care about your debt and overspending because the world will not know about it. Your debt or your budget is your prerogative. Many people are walking around living with debt silently. That is why it does not benefit us in the long run to keep up with the Joneses because the Joneses could be drowning in debt. Trying to keep up with others and trends has a subtle element of truth in it, which many people having become victim of coveting what others have. Only to find out later that bills, debt, sickness, stress accompany excessive spending and borrowing money. Debt can be a silent killer. It has caused many celebrities to commit suicide and many celebrities have died broke or in significant debt despite earning hundreds of millions of dollars. Debt does not discriminate. Many people that are rich do not do a good job of controlling their wants because they cannot control their desires. There are others that use their riches for altruistic purposes.

United States is one of the few countries that have a culture that looks forward to kicking their children out of the parents' home at eighteen years old. Young adults should be encouraged to stay at home and go to school and work to save money as long as they follow a life or budget plan agreed upon by the parents. The young adults must have financial goals in mind and be diligently working towards achieving them. I encourage parents to provide your children as much support as they need in this ever changing economic environment. Then release them into the wild when they are mature and ready to fend for themselves while continuing to save money.

Society tells us we should have certain things that we may not necessarily need, at least not immediately or impulsively. Sometimes our lack of planning and processing our purchasing decisions cause extra duress than we need. Strongly consider putting a financial plan in place to save cash and live well below your income to live comfortably.

Save Cash

CARD SERVICES™
⬛⬛⬛ardservices.com

KEVIN D POWELL

ǁդǁɿǁǁɿɔɔɹɿǁɹդɿդɿդդɿդɿɔɔɹɹɹɿɿɿɹɔɿɿɔɔɹɿɿǁǁǁɿɿ

February 24, 2012

Regarding account number ending in: ⬛⬛⬛

Dear Kevin D Powell:

This letter confirms that the above referenced account has been closed, as you requested   Please cancel any scheduled automatic payments through Online Banking.

Please destroy all credit cards associated with this account by cutting the magnetic strip in half. Also, dispose of any cash advance checks. Please be sure to notify those companies that may post recurring charges to the account to pay for products and services such as Internet access, health club memberships, and subscriptions, that the account is closed.

For general information about your balance, payments, and available credit, or to speak with a customer satisfaction associate about reopening the account, please call 1.800⬛⬛⬛. We are at your service 24 hours a day, seven days a week. We value your business and hope we can be of service in the future.

Sincerely,

⬛⬛⬛

Customer Satisfaction Department

42 Precepts of Maat

1. I have not done what is wrong.
2. I have not robbed with violence.
3. I have not done violence.
4. I have not committed theft.
5. I have not murdered man or woman.
6. I have not defrauded offerings.
7. I have not acted deceitfully.
8. I have not robbed the things that belong to God.
9. I have told no lies.
10. I have not snatched away food.
11. I have not uttered evil words.
12. I have attacked no one.
13. I have not slaughtered the sacred Bull.
14. I have not laid waste the ploughed lands.
15. I have not eaten my heart.
16. I have not been an eavesdropper.
17. I have not spoken against anyone.
18. I have not become angry without just cause.
19. I have not committed adultery.
20. I have not committed any sin against my own purity.
21. I have not violated sacred times and seasons.
22. I have not done that which is abominable.
23. I have not uttered fiery words.
24. I have not stopped my ears from listening to words of right and wrong.
25. I have not stirred up strife.
26. I have not caused anyone to weep.
27. I have not lusted, committed fornication, or laid with others of my same sex.
28. I have not avenged myself.
29. I have not worked grief, I have not abused anyone.

30. I have not acted insolently or with violence.
31. I have not judged hastily.
32. I have not transgressed or angered God.
33. I have not talked too much.
34. I have not done harm or evil.
35. I have not worked treason or curses on the King.
36. I have never befouled the water.
37. I have not spoken scornfully.
38. I have not cursed The God.
39. I have not behaved with arrogance.
40. I have not been overwhelmingly proud or sought distinctions for myself.
41. I have not desired more than what is rightfully mine.
42. I have never blasphemed The God in my native town.

AUTHOR'S COMMENTARY

Gen Xers are the first generation to have a significant number of both parents working outside of the home. After the Civil Rights Act of 1964, masses of women entered the workforce. Daycare business grew in popularity and children were placed in daycare or left with grandparents. However, African Americans had a large percentage of both parents working out of the home and children were left with family members like grandparents or great aunts. I am part of the generation X age group that likes work/life balance and spending time with my family. I feel strongly that children should have at least one parent at home while the other parent is working. If both parents work then they should be left with a responsible elderly family member, instead of being placed in a daycare. Xer's like to have options, i.e. flex time and the option to work from home or in an office. I believe generation Xers are the way they are because they witnessed their parents work long hours, which was similar to abandonment. Consequently, the children of baby boomer decided they would spend as much time with their children as they could.

That separation must have created the thought process in their children to work from home, pick up the children, attend sporting events, and have dinner together. It rubbed off on me because I have avoided opportunities that would require me to work 10-14 hour days and neglect spending time with my family. These are things young people growing up who will become future leaders have to consider. They have to decide what works best for them and their family. And, it is not all about making a lot of money when you are not happy in your family life. You have to have and maintain balance for harmony in your life and relationships.

QUOTES

Money doesn't grow on trees is an absolute statement. KP

If you never thought saving money was critical, think again. It is vitally important now and forever; cash is still king in the physical world. KP

Saving money is mandatory for wealth creation. The more you save the better your living condition will be in the long-term. Know this, if you don't save, you will be sorry when you need the money the most. KP

Why is the gap widening between the rich and the poor in the 21st century, when it is considered the knowledge age of 24 hours x 7 days a week access to a super information highway and educational advancement? Where has the American dream gone wrong for 99% of Americans? The dream is available to anyone if they become educated about money, earn a living, and commit to saving money. KP

118

*Make a commitment to save: pay yourself out of everything
you earn. Once it is saved, don't turn around and
spend it frivolously. KP*

*The poor and middle-class are too quick to put their children
out of the house. Americans are known for doing that to their
children. Instead, parents should help their children get up on
their feet with a solid financial foundation
before pushing them out of the nest. KP*

*"My own experience in the third world was that even if people
started to make more money, the cost of living and housing
increased often faster than the wages." David Korten*

"Lack of Money is trouble without equal." Rabelais (1534)

Be persistent and steady like the turtle in the race. KP

*Give yourself positive affirmations daily; as an example, I feel
and know the difference between my desires and my needs. KP*

Peace,

Kevin Powell
Copyright 2012

www.ingramcontent.com/pod-product-compliance
Lightning Source LLC
Chambersburg PA
CBHW071601200326
41519CB00021BB/6831